YOUR
ROUTE
TO SUCCESS

BOZIDAR BARRY STRK

Copyright © 2013 **Bozidar Barry Strk**
All rights reserved.

ISBN: 1494212382
ISBN 13: 9781494212384

Library of Congress Control Number: 2013921493
**CreateSpace Independent Publishing Platform,
North Charleston, South Carolina**

This page I dedicate to my parents;

ANTE (Tony) and DINKA STRK

Who grew up in Eastern Europe under communist control. They were poor, but proud, self reliant, resilient, resourceful, with a can do attitude, who worked very hard on the small parcels of land they owned to provide for their family. I remember that somehow they always managed to make ends meet with out the help of any Government programs.

(It really is sad that about fifty years later in the greatest and the richest country in the world the U.S.A. that far too many of our fellow citizens rely on some kind of taxpayers subsidized program).

I attribute my success in business and my personal and family life to their beliefs and teachings. As I was growing up they thought me; about work ethic, responsibility, honesty, reliability, being respectful, frugal, self-reliance, optimistic, persistent, family values, faith, power of prayer and the trust in God. Yes the trust in God, and this is many years before they ever saw an America Dollar with the words; IN GOD WE TRUST.

Not a day passes by that I don't think about both of them, especially my mother who passed away at only fifty-two years old. God bless her soul and may she rest in peace. My father is eighty-two years old and living in Croatia, town of Kukljica near city of Zadar located on a beautiful Adriatic Sea coastline. He still does organic gardening and takes care of many olive trees, as he continues the family tradition of making the olive oil. Olive oil so good that many European Vacationers say, it may be the best olive oil in the world due to the Adriatic Sea climate. Visit Croatia's coastline that is blessed with awesome natural beauty and decide for yourself.

THANK YOU MOM and DAD

Thanks to you, and all of your teaching's, believes, family values and faith in God that I can pass it down to my own children every single day to make a positive difference in their lives and one day their children's lives.

GOD BLESS.

ACKNOWLEDGEMENTS

Through out the book I stress the point of how nothing great or worthwhile is achieved overnight, with ease, and all by yourself. Same implies in writing this book. I don't even know the number of times I rewrote each chapter. Typing on computer, which was a challenge in itself since I haven't done any major typing from the days I would correct my typing mistakes by the white out, and patiently wait for it to dry before I would proceed. Now you can tell that I needed help to get started and to finish the book. Thankfully I got the help I needed and now is the time to acknowledge this and thank them. It's a right thing to do.

I wish to thank my sons Dennis and Allen for their patience in teaching me not only how to type on the computer but also the workings of the computer as well as positives and negatives of Internet. My niece Sandy for all the encouragement to keep going, when the going got tough. Elio Klaric, friend and co-worker for many years. Simply put all around great family man and true professional route owner/operator who was there for me when ever I needed advice. I can't forget my wife Marina for her patience and her help with my project, as I had papers scattered all over the house for many months. Authors Cheryl Lodico and Mary Mihaly who not only gave me advice about their experiences of writing and publishing their books but also made me feel that I can do this. With projects such as this were you get help and advice from many people you tend to forget some of them. To them all I can say I am sorry and I will make it up to you.

Acknowledgements

Message to the reader.

This book contains the opinions and ideas of it's author. It is intended to provide helpful and informative material on the subjects addressed in this book. It is sold with the understanding that the author and the publisher are not engaged in rendering any personal or professional advice or business services.

The author and the publisher specifically disclaim all responsibility for any liability, loss, or risk personal or otherwise, which is incurred as a consequences, directly or indirectly of the use and application of any of the contents in this book.

CONTENTS

Introduction

Chapter One
Life is full of choices?

Chapter Two
Why do so many people want to run their own business?

Chapter Three
What is a Route Business?

Chapter Four
What types of routes are there?

Chapter Five
Which Route Business to buy?

Chapter Six
Is buying a Route Business in tough economy a bad decision?

Chapter Seven
How much can I expect to make owning and operating a Route Business? Is it a good investment?

Chapter Eight
Advantages and some challenges of route ownership?

Chapter Nine
Where can I buy the Route Business?

Chapter Ten
Responsibilities of a route owner?

Chapter Eleven
Do I need prior route business experience to be successful?

Chapter Twelve
How much money do I need to buy a route? What is the best way to finance the purchase?

Chapter Thirteen
Ways to save for a down payment on the purchase of a Route Business or any other small business, or a big-ticket item.

Chapter Fourteen
In the event I get sick or I want to go on a vacation, who will take care of my Route Business?

Chapter Fifteen
Do most Route Businesses include the vehicle? Where do I keep the vehicle? Do I need a special license to drive?

Chapter Sixteen
Money saving tips on vehicle insurance.

Chapter Seventeen
Questions you must answer before you start looking to buy a route?

Chapter Eighteen
A commitment and a promise to yourself, on start looking to buy a route, or any other small business.

Chapter Nineteen
A sample of questions and personal information you will be asked for, when you are ready to purchase a Route Business.

Chapter Twenty
How to increase your weekly sales, which in turn you will make more money every week, and increase the value of your route business?

Chapter Twenty One
Your route to success depends on you staying healthy, optimistic, and positive, in a very competitive market place.

Chapter Twenty Two
My recollection of the two terrorist attacks on the World Trade Center Complex, while servicing the accounts inside.

Chapter Twenty Three
Don't buy a route business if?

Chapter Twenty Four
My secrets to success. A special bonus chapter, as a thank you for purchasing the book, and my sincere hope and best wishes on "YOUR ROUTE TO SUCCESS."

Chapter Twenty Five
My distributor of the year award.

Chapter Twenty Six
Financial growth chart.

Chapter Twenty Seven
Reaching a point of financial independence and having enough.

Chapter Twenty Eight
Your thought's and beliefs, before reading the book.

Chapter Twenty Nine
Your thought's and beliefs after reading the book.

Chapter Thirty
Concluding thoughts.

Chapter Thirty One
List of Major Companies that sell routes/distributorships

INTRODUCTION

My name is Bozidar Barry Strk, the route expert. I loved the route business so much and when you love something and do it for over twenty years you do become expert at it. I thank you for your interest in a route business. My decision in writing this book is a way to giveback, to somehow, in someway, return the favor to the people who have helped me on my long journey to a better life for my family and me. It was also a personal challenge to put my; discipline, confidence, and can-do positive attitude to test in writing this book. While spending countless hours in writing and many times rewriting this book, thought of, "What's in it for me? What do I get out of this? "Never crossed my mind. After so many months of diligently working on this project, it's still is about; to give back, to help, to teach, to inspire, all those who choose this route to success.

What's in it for me, in writing this book are rewards; of personal pride, satisfaction of knowing, that not only I am trying to help people better their lives, but at the same time improving my own life. Using my discipline, confidence and a can-do positive attitude every day on this-the very meaningful and personal project. Discovering and proving to myself; that I can write the book, I can learn about the complex world of book editing, publishing, and marketing. These are the benefits that you can't put the price on, as well as joyful contentment, and satisfaction, after many, many, months writing this book that I can say; "I did it, I gave it my best."

If you would thoroughly know anything, teach it to others.

Tyron Edwards
American theologian

Introduction

My goal in writing this book is to truly help you to explain and succeed in the route business. I will try my very best to totally, honestly and sincerely describe my twenty-one years of successfully owning and operating a Pepperidge Farm Cookies and Crackers Route in N.Y.C. There are many different local and national brand name products routes you can buy. Selling bread, cookies, potato chips, pretzels, soda, juices, cold cuts (provisions), candy, and many others. Prior to owning a route business I had two retail gourmet chocolate, candy, ice cream and cookie shops in N.Y.C. area. I also worked for Pepsi Cola Bottling Company of N.Y. as a district manager. My plan was always to work for myself and be my own boss. I am a self starter, go getter with a can - do attitude, self confidence, discipline, desire, and a need to grow, improve, and work hard for a better tomorrow. I love the route business because it offers so much to individual owner operator. It gives you the flexibility to buy a large or small route business and to be able to work three days a week or four, five and six. Part time or full time with a starting and quitting time of your choosing.

Steady and predictable weekly income (with small weekly variance depending on sales.]

No employees

No store or warehouse

No franchise fees or royalty payments

Low start up and overhead expenses

Job security

Route business provides an immediate and secured steady income. In most cases people buy already established route. The seller may be retiring or purchasing a larger route. Whatever the reason you will spend time with a seller (at least two weeks) so you will know average weekly sales the route generates, all the expenses and profit. More important you will find out and see how the route is operated and learn first hand can you do this and would like to do it. Even more importantly you will find out can you see yourself in doing this ten years from now. Also the parent company of the products you will be selling and distributing will provide you with average weekly sales volume the route is generating for the last six to twelve months. In most cases they will break it down to what each account on the route is averaging in weekly sales for last six to twelve months. It's a great, comfortable reassuring feeling to know what your weekly take home money would be should you decide to buy a route business. There are not many businesses' that you can start that can just about guarantee you weekly take home earnings and a long-term success. It's a very simple basic business to operate and expand it, to make more money, and if you wish sell the route with substantial gain. Then you can buy a bigger route and possibly hire a helper to run your route, while you spend more time growing and expanding the business.

Another great thing about the route business is the freedom that it offers you as far as the time and days you go out to work. Most of you know the saying, N.Y.C. is the city that never sleeps. The majority of my small convenience stores on the route in N.Y.C. were open twenty-four hours seven days a week. N.Y.C. like most big cities has the rush hour traffic, congestion and parking nightmares. So the best and most efficient way to manage my time is to go to work very early and that meant three o'clock in the morning. I would finish my day by noon to one o clock in the afternoon. This way I would avoid the morning and evening rush hour. Any day I had to come home earlier or simply take day off I would work longer day before and day after. You don't want to lose any sales, remember you are working for yourself on commission basis. I call the route business as close to a guaranteed success as in any business you can think off. To make the projected weekly earnings on the route you are buying you simply have to copy the seller's work and effort. To make more money then the seller plan to work little harder, longer, smarter, offer better service, open new accounts, put up more promotional displays and what ever else you have to do to increase the sales. You have the choice; it's all up to you. You are in control, your own boss. Your future, financial security your success is in your hands. If this is what you dreamed, wished and hoped for then I can tell you from my own experience the route business is a perfect small business for you.

To be successful at it, you must have a great work habit, be a self starter, disciplined, with positive attitude, confidence in yourself and products you are selling, reliable, responsible and naturally be able to work and get along with people. People such as store owners, managers, assistant managers, receivers and your own parent company district manager, warehouse manager where you will pick the product from, and your fellow route owners they are all important to get along with for your long term success.

Your route business expenses are basically your truck expenses gas repairs insurance. Depending on which route you buy there might be also some warehouse expenses where you pick up and also may store extra product you ordered for special promotion.

This perfect small business for owner operator will give you a great sense of job and income security, which now counts so much more then ever before as globalization has greatly diminished the number of quality high paying jobs along with job security in general.

I will try my very best to help, guide, motivate, inspire and teach you to be the best that you can be in your route business. When you do something successfully for twenty-one years like I have, you do become very good at it, an expert in the field. I wish you lots of good luck and much success on your journey to route ownership and on YOUR ROUTE TO SUCCESS.

Chapter 1
LIFE IS FULL OF CHOICES:

#1 CONTINUE WITH YOUR LIFE?

- Blame others for lack of success
- Work at the dead end job
- Go nowhere financially
- Sit on the couch watch T.V.
- Buy a lottery ticket and dream

OR

#2 TAKE CHARGE OF YOUR LIFE, YOUR FUTURE AND FINANCIAL SECURITY?

- Invest in yourself
- Be in control of your money NOT the Wall St. Bankers
- Learn how to own and operate a route business

Life Is Full Of Choices:

- Produce income and build wealth

- GET RICH SLOW, STEADY and SECURELY OVER TIME

    IT'S   ALL   UP   TO   YOU?

If you don't have enough money, for your own business, read the chapter on; Ways to save for down payment on the route business or any other small business.

According to the U.S. Census Bureau the number of self-employed people, grew from 15.4 million to nearly 21million between 1997 and 2006.

Many people dream of owning their business.

WHY STRUGGLE TO THE TOP IN SOMEONE ELSE'S BUSINESS, WHEN YOU CAN START AT THE TOP IN YOU OWN.

This guide is dedicated to all of those whose wishes; hopes, and dreams, are of working for themselves, and being their own boss, by owning a small business and people who strongly believe in self reliance, NOT government, family, or relatives dependence. What build and made America the most powerful, the richest and the most generous nation in the world is honest hard work, necessary sacrifices and personal responsibility. Buying only what you need and can afford not what you want. With growing number of our citizens relying on, ever increasing subsidized programs that has our country so overextended financially that is threatening American quality of life along with the American Dream for so many.

We have always been a nation of self-help people. At the beginning of our democracy everyone provided for themselves and their families. Nobody expected to be taken care of, or think that they were entitled to something for nothing. What defined America and what we stood for was; independence, freedom, pride and self –reliance. As tough economic times came along, with very competitive Global Market Place, and more subsidized programs to rely on, we started to loose it.

My wish and hope in writing this book is to reverse this trend and offer the people an opportunity for self-reliance, independence and all the freedom that comes with it. In this book you will learn of all the advantages of owning you own business (route business or any other small business.] You will get the knowledge and learn to acquire success habits that lead you to path of American Dream and financial independence. It's about helping-teaching, motivating and inspiring you to learn how to work for yourself by owning a small business and succeed at it.

Learning how to work smarter by yourself and for yourself. A genuine opportunity to learn and earn more with no get rich quick schemes, lies or empty promises. My goal and objective is to help and guide you to get there by owning a route business or simply to read the book and understand it completely and its message through out the book, especially the chapter on; My secrets to success. As I am writing this book and the time when you read it, there will be people in many poor countries, either planning to come here or already on their way to America. They are risking their lives, either crossing the ocean in a small boat or walking across the deserts of Arizona and Texas the sad part is that many do loose their life. They simply want a chance an opportunity for a better life here in America. Millions, who come here legally or illegally, do any kind of work that they can find, usually the worst, the hardest, and the lowest paying jobs. They don't work the regular five days and hours of nine to five, its more like six or seven days ten to twelve hours a day. They work, eat and sleep and do it again and again and again. Total dedication and discipline, until they learn the language and acquire skills, that enable them to move on to better jobs, with better pay and improved working conditions.

When you adopt their total dedication, self-discipline, and work habit and all the sacrifices they make, you develop a kind of mind set that in time you will and must succeed with out any doubt in my mind.

All of you who are born here in this, the greatest country in the world of ours, you have so many advantages over the recent immigrants that is impossible to list them all. So I will just list the few;

You are born here, your family, relatives, friends; your total support group is here. You know the language, you went to school here, you have safe clean home to come to, with variety of food available like nowhere else in the world. My God, this is your country. Period.

Yet so many of us are in debt and living pay check to pay check, not to mention the millions who cant find a job and the millions more who rely on help and programs of some kind or the other from the government. Yet the immigrants are still somewhere planning or are already on their way to America. Some come legally, but many come illegally. Number of them paid the smugglers everything of the very little they had saved to come here, and many others are risking their lives to come.

Do you ever ask yourself?

What do they know about America that we don't know?

What do they see in America that we don't see?

What have they heard about America that we did not hear?

Are they smarter, stronger, or better-looking, do they see or hear better then us?

Why is their belief in America so strong and so confident?

What is it, that makes them leave their country, their family, relatives, friends, their way of life and then on top of all that, put their life in jeopardy just to come to America. Maybe, just maybe, they are told our streets are paved with gold and the rush is on. Once they get here they quickly discover that streets are not paved with gold, but instead with the opportunity to work and buy gold. Its very simple, work hard and over time you will succeed, if you want something bad enough.

The reality is many of our citizens choose not to want it bad enough, (the self reliance, success, financial independence, and a pride of providing for you and your family) rather they just chose to rely on the government help for its many subsidized programs.

HERE IS THE GOOD NEWS FOR YOU.

The good news is that you have a complete control of your thoughts, habits decisions, actions and inactions you take. We posses this great power which we take for granted and rarely stop and think about.

Only you have the power to change your life for the better. I can only show you, and make you aware of the many different paths and actions you need to take.

Every person in his or her life experiences, the ups and downs. How well and how quickly you change and adopt determines your success or a failure. You should consider yourself your own boss, with the power to make the decisions about what's best for you and what plan of action you need to take to reach your goals and succeed.

I can never forget the people who helped me along the way to my own American Dream and Financial Independence. My purpose in writing this book is to help you to be better and succeed.

Success is right here, right now, (the streets may not be paved with gold, but they are with an opportunity to work and buy gold.} The sad part is more and more people simply fail to go for it, with a deep burning desire, positive attitude, work ethic, self-discipline, personal responsibility and are unwilling to make the necessary sacrifices that American Dream requires us to have and make to be able to achieve it.

NOTHING WORTHWHILE IS ACHIEVED OVER NIGHT AND WITH EASE.

The reality is if you don't see or choose not to see the streets that are paved with gold, there are many more immigrants who are planning right now to come to the streets that they see as paved with gold.

"Reflection of our lives depends on the choices we make. To have a better life, simply make better choices." I really do hope and wish that you do make better choices and succeed in you own way. Good luck.

6 | Life Is Full Of Choices:

We need eagles

A shell gives turtle warmth and security. He has no foes, no cares, nothing to strive for.

The eagle flies through the heavens screaming defiance to the elements. Aroused he is formidable. The eagle, not the turtle, is America's symbol.

Source unknown

If I may speak for all the route owners, other small business owners, self-employed individuals, and many others across the country, who have view's and believes; in hard work, personal responsibility, family values, and self-reliance, that we are all proud American Eagles. Every single day we make America, a better place to be.

American Character

Americanism means the virtues of courage, honor, justice, truth, sincerity and hardihood-the virtues that made America great. The things that will destroy America are prosperity-at-any price, safety first instead of duty first, the love of soft living and the get-rich-quick theory of life.

Theodore Roosevelt
Twenty-sixth president of the United States

Chapter 2

WHY DO SO MANY PEOPLE WANT TO RUN THEIR OWN BUSINESS?[1]

Think and write down of all the reasons you want to run yours. I am sure their reasons are pretty much, the same reasons as yours.

Intuit, the makers of Quick Books and other business products, and services surveyed 1,000 people, ages twenty- five to fifty – five, about starting their own businesses. They learned that about three-quarters of Americans see owning a home or business as the "American Dream," while 84 percent thought that if they started their own business, they would be more passionate about their work.

More then a third regretted not starting their own business.

Their primary reasons for wanting to start a business included:

- 40 percent wanted to love their work.

- 24 percent wanted to be their own boss.

- 21 percent wanted more flexible schedules.

- 15 percent wanted to spend more time with their families.

---

1 The 250 Questions Every Self-Employed Person Should Ask by Mary Mihaly

They have a dream, they have a passion they want to follow and work at every day, and they hate having a boss. They want to set their own hours, make their own rules, and develop their own work relationships. Reap all the benefits from their ideas and hard work, not someone else.

Why struggle to the top in someone else's business when you can start at the top in your own?

You're still there. Working hard. Staying late. Seeking recognition. Worrying about job security. You're willing to put in the extra hours it takes to build a more rewarding future. Coming home after a long, grueling day, you sometimes wonder if there isn't a better way. If you're working hard now, why shouldn't you be rewarded now?

You should.

And you can be, by owning a Route Business or any other small business. Fellow readers I know of no secret or a magic formula for success. I only know you have to not only work hard, but work smart, for yourself, and over time success will be yours.

OVER THE YEARS COMPANIES SELLING BRAND NAME ROUTES HAVE PERFECTED DISTRIBUTION, SALES, AND TRAINING TECHNIQUES THAT TAKE THE GUESSWORK, OR ANY DOUBTS OUT OF RUNNING YOUR OWN ROUTE BUSINESS SUCCESSFULLY. THIS IS THE REASON THAT I CALL IT A PROVEN PLAN TO SUCCEED.

There is virtually no limits on your success, but it all depends on how hard, how smart, and how big is your desire to succeed. There are thousands of route owners across the country that love the Route Business so much, that they bought additional routes. It all depends on your own initiative and ambition. It's a down-to earth business that can make you very successful.

You are the embodiment of the information you choose to accept and act upon. To change your circumstances you need to change your thinking and subsequent actions.

Adlin Sinclair

Today's workplace is far from a happy and secured one.

If you have a secured job, that you are truly satisfied and happy with, I congratulate you. Today's job reality is that you are in the minority of our work force who fall in that category. The voices of the majority workers can be heard saying;
"I worry about my job."
"What job security."
"I know it's a dead end job."
"I work because I have to."
"My boss doesn't appreciate me or my work."
"All they care is about profit and their shareholders not their workers."
"I can't afford to loose this job."
"I am discouraged and frustrated."
"I live paycheck to paycheck."
"They made record profit and still laid people off."
"Even when working overtime I still don't make enough."
"After years of working I never seem to get ahead."
"I find it difficult to save for my retirement."
"I get angry, because I feel I am kind of trapped."
"There are not many jobs out there."
"I don't have control of my life or my future."
"I wish I could start my own business."

  These are the voices, feelings, and concerns of real people. They could be your friends, your neighbors, and your co-workers. Many of the statements may relate to you and your family.

  I personally know the feeling and I can truly sympathize with them as my wife lost her job after working for twenty years in the bank. It's painful and very personal, especially after so many years. My wife worked very hard and did everything they asked of her and more. Suddenly they turned her world upside down as there was no warning or notice of any kind. Then she started asking questions; Why me? What did I do wrong? What didn't I do? "I always tried my best and did all they asked of me." "Maybe my supervisor or a district manager didn't like me"? "Maybe they will assign my work on to the other workers or hire a college graduate, train him or her for a much smaller pay." Just by looking and talking to my wife I could tell she was upset, so naturally it affected me as well. My reasoning, assuring, and explaining to her that we will be fine, made things easier and made the positive difference. The real deep down difference was that I owned a small business (Route Business) that was secure and consistent for over twenty years, as well as over the years we were both disciplined in saving for our retirement and put funds on the side for situations like this. We also never liked being in debt, so thankfully we were debt free. Over time the shock, the disappointment and some anger over loosing her job slowly disappeared.

The unpleasant memories of loosing your job stay with you all your life. Fellow readers I don't like to be negative, but the fact and reality is, that at times for far too many of us it's a cruel, cruel, world out there.

Often it seems that it's all about profit, and at all cost profit. Your hard work, good will, and your loyalty of ten or twenty years and more, no longer count, they don't mean a thing, it's all forgotten, like you never worked there, almost like you no longer exist.

With periods of economic turmoil in different parts of the world, rampant merger and acquisition activity, and intense focus on increased productivity, improved performance, can anyone feel truly secure in a job or a career today?

One of the reasons that I have decided to write this book, is to inform as many people as I possibly can about this great small business (The Route Business) and all the advantages that it offers. Maybe, I can help you change that cruel, cruel, world to a better, more secure, and happy one.

Owning a Route Business you no longer have the many worries and concerns as you do with working for somebody else. It's a whole new and exciting ballgame. A ballgame where you are the leader, the #1 Star, were you create and make things happen.

Your job, your career, your business is secured.
Going to work can be fun, meaningful, and satisfying again.
From the first day, your work will make the positive difference in your life.
Now you work matters, a great deal, day in and day out.
Your work is challenging, exciting, and never boring.
Not only is it rewarding financially, but emotionally and physically as well.
You feel proud, independent, and self-reliant.
You like your new business, you are committed, and intend to be the best that you can be at it, after all it's yours.
Suddenly you look forward and enjoying going to work, to build, to create, and succeed.
Operating a Route Business it helps you in building; self-discipline, self-confidence, and a can-do attitude.
It's also comforting and assuring to know that when things do get challenging that you are not by yourself. The company management team is your support group, your guide, and your coach, there to help you to grow your business and succeed. When you succeed, they do as well.
You get the great feeling and satisfaction of being in charge of your life, and your future.

Good luck on your journey to a better future for you and your family.

Chapter 3
WHAT IS A ROUTE BUSINESS?

Your morning toast, bagel, orange juice, yogurt, and the afternoon snacks like potato chips, cookies, pretzels, beverages, and many more items do not just appear out of nowhere at your local supermarket or a convenience store. Someone has to deliver it, put it on the stores shelves, and take out any old product that is out of date to be sold by. This someone is a route owner, who in most cases gets up very early in the morning to bring you the freshest product possible while you are still at sleep. They really are the unsung heroes of the food industry, who day in and day out under all kinds of weather conditions bring you the fresh quality products that you and me the consumers demand.

Route Business is basically a distributor's, direct store delivery (D S D). You have a van, step van or a truck (which usually comes with a purchase of a route business) and it's loaded with product such as bread cookies, potato chips, beverages etc. Your job is to deliver, service and sell to stores and other retail accounts. Some routes have exclusive protected territories, which are described in your contract or a distributorship agreement with a parent company. What that means is that in the territory area in your contract gives you the exclusive rights to sell their products to all the stores located in only that area. You cannot sell their products outside that area and nobody else can come to sell their products in you described area. Where some other routes have protected accounts, so when you purchase this particular route your contract or a distributorship agreement instead of having a description of your exclusive territory it will have a list of stores that are exclusively yours to deliver and sell their products to them. This is why I mentioned earlier before you buy any route business you must spend (full time) at least two weeks or more with an owner operator (the seller) and learn, write notes and see how he runs the route. Observe what kind of person, a businessman he is, what his area and his accounts are like. How does he get along with storeowners, managers, and receivers? Are they happy to see him or they complain about him? How well does he sell and merchandise his products?

As a route owner or a distributor, you own a business that generates income for you and your family. Your distributorship is a lot more than a job. It is an investment you made which requires dedication, day-to-day focus, attention to detail, and consistent service to all your accounts. Whatever the accounts needs are. Stores cannot be out stock of your brand name products. As a route owner you have a great deal of flexibility in running your route. Your parent company's salesman or a district manager will guide and help you increase your profitability by teaching you the best practices used by thousands of route owners like yourself. The route ownership is a partnership between you and a parent company. When your business grows so does theirs. The nationally recognized brand name products you will be selling all ready have a reputation for quality and consumer acceptance, which will make it so much easier to sell.

Real key to success is you, the distributor providing the consistent service to all your stores day in and day out.

As a distributor you are in a position to benefit from the best, of two worlds. On one hand you're part of a distribution and sales team for a successful brand name nationally known company. On the other hand you're an independent businessperson, able to utilize company's investments in marketing, research, sales technology and support resources to grow your business. The company relies upon you to deliver the products and offer best service to all your stores. A customer who is disappointed with the lack of availability of product or its freshness wont understand that the problem was just on this route. He or she will attribute the problem to the company as a whole and make the next buying decision accordingly. When you purchase your route you start a business, which is more than a job. A job implies limited responsibility and opportunities; where as your route

14 | What Is A Route Business?

ownership and its association with the parent company offers you greater flexibility. Using your creativity and consistent service to increase sales and grow your business.

As a route owner (or DSD distributor), you are running a small business and are responsible for the amount of sales volume you generate and the earnings you can enjoy. Just about all routes work this way. You pick up the product from the parent company's warehouse what ever you need for that day depending on the product, or it may be for a whole week sales to your stores. You pay for the product at the end of the week or in most cases next week for last weeks order. Most all chain stores are preapproved for credit by the parent company so you make the delivery, get the stores manager or a receiver signature and a store stamp on your delivery invoice and you are ready for next account. All deliveries to small convenience store, known in the route business as (cash stores) you collect C.O.D. It is up to you as a route owner if you wish to extend any credit to small stores or any accounts that are not approved for credit by the parent company. In my own twenty one years of experience just about all small stores were C.O.D. Situations did come up where I just came to service the store and owner just paid out large amount of money for cigarette or a beer delivery the he would ask me for credit for few days or until next weeks delivery. You know it's a good store you have been servicing it for period of time and he is low on your product, why loose the sale. I would give him the order and collect the payment on the time we agreed on.

You are here to sell and grow the business. Any lost sales are lost forever as is your commission. By extending credit in such circumstances, at the same time you also build a good will with a storeowner. Who is also in the business to make a profit and keep his store shelves well stocked with quality fast selling products like yours and keep his customers happy. Nobody likes to shop in the store that has empty shelves, like he is going out the business. Many of the small independent stores chose to pay for their order by check. It's very important to make sure they made check payable to you or your corporation if you chose to incorporate your route business. (Whether to incorporate or not it depends on so many factors its best to discuss it with your own accountant. In my own experience majority of route owners did not incorporate.]

I would hand the invoice with big Pepperidge Farm name and its logos that company supplies us with. The printer in the step van would print out the invoice with route owners name or corporation name in much smaller print and storeowner would not notice it and make the check payable to Pepperidge Farm.

Pepperidge Farm (as well as most other large companies) does not accept, third party checks. Like any other business you have to stay focused, organized and be detail oriented to make your job more easier, rewarding and more profitable.

Chapter 4
WHAT TYPES OF ROUTES ARE THERE?

There are many types of routes you can buy. These include; bread, cookies, beverage, snacks, cake, pretzels, dairy, coffee catering, vending, provisions, ice cream, newspaper, Fed Ex, office and window cleaning and more. Some of these are nationally recognized brand name routes. They usually cost a lot more then the ones that are regional or local routes, which are called Independent Routes. Nationally recognized brand name routes usually you can only sell their product from the vehicle you are using to service the stores. While Independent Routes you can sell many different products from many manufacturers. You can also buy product from more than one supplier. Independent Routes may include cake, meat, dairy, provisions, bread routes and more. Brand name routes usually have geographic territorial boundaries, or protected accounts that belong to your route and only you can service them.

Since I owned and successfully operated a brand name route I am definitely in favor of buying a brand name route, a route with geographical territorial boundaries rather than protected accounts. I also have an experience in starting my own small business distributing specialty candy, chocolates, nuts and dried fruits, cookies and holiday novelties to specialty candy and gourmet stores through out the N.Y.C. area. I was competing with possibly dozen or more distributors selling same and similar items to mostly same stores. It was extremely competitive and not even close to financially rewarding as owning and operating a brand name route business. Like the saying goes "You get what you pay for." Owning a brand name route you have the nationally famous, quality products that consumer wants and product sells itself, period. You have the protected territory or protected accounts, which nobody can sell that product to them but you. How much simpler or easier can it be? Brand name route you are buying is an already established business. You will spend time (at least two weeks or more) full time on the route with the seller. This is the way to learn the route, to actually be there every step of the way. From taking the order in the store, putting it together in the truck, delivering it to the store, getting the order checked in and putting it on the shelves of your section in the store and promotional displays if you placed any previously. Chain stores usually have the receivers who checked the order in sign and stamp the invoice or sign the screen on your hand held computer.

With smaller stores, you collect the payment due C.O.D. There is no negotiating or haggling over the prices as you are charging the same prices as previous route owner. Storeowner knows that is the price and he can only get that product from you. On occasion I heard of some route owners who tried to overcharge smaller stores, but eventually storeowner would find out through other storeowners or friends in the business that they are being overcharged. Then storeowner may stop selling your product, or demand a free order and call your district manager if situation is not resolved fairly. Route owners like these usually don't last long in the route business. Successful route owners are honest, hard working day in and day out, helpful, dedicated, sincere individuals who plan their work and work their plan every day. They get to know storeowners and managers on first name basis and develop friendships after serving their store for several years on weekly basis.

If I had to buy a route all over again I would buy again a brand name route and protected territory like I had with Pepperidge Farm. There are some disadvantages to this but in my opinion and my experience the overall advantages by far surpass the disadvantages. Main disadvantage is that you are limited to sell your product only to your described area, or protected accounts. Strong discipline, patience and hard work, build and grow your area to its outmost potential. After you called on every single potential customer in your area, and you are providing absolute best service to all your accounts you still want to grow and have need to make more money.

18 | What Types Of Routes Are There?

Make an appointment with your area or district manager to go with you on the route. Most national companies with brand name routes have the area or district manager whose primary job is to help the route owners grow the business. Most independent routes don't have the managers to help and guide you and your business and make more money.

Very simply two heads are smarter then one in anything you are trying to accomplish. You might be pleasantly surprised of sales opportunities your area manager may find on your route. After an area manager is working with you on the route and finds you really are an excellent route owner/salesman and there is very little opportunity for growth, then he or she will try their best to help you to buy additional territory that borders your area or additional protected accounts close to your existing accounts. There might be a chance one neighboring route owner has too much to handle (maybe a big chain store opened recently in his area or he is getting older and would like to work less or possibly somebody with a bigger route may be moving or retiring.) This is where your patience, discipline and staying focused on continuing doing excellent job on your route comes into account. This may take six months to one or two years. Since you want to expand and need to make more money my guess is, you already like the route business you have decided to make a career out of it. Waiting six months to two years for something you really like and want to do for next ten to twenty years or more and make the income you want, the job security it provides is not such a long time.

Route business, especially name brand with quality products and an excellent reputation you must learn to look at the long-term picture. While on my own route I got to know many route owners who were with the company fifteen, twenty, thirty years and more. Some were working in their late sixties. Not because they had to do it for financial reasons. They did it because they loved the route business. Most of them as they got older sold part of their route, so instead of working five days they worked instead three to four days. It's a beautiful feeling to know you are in control of this very important decision, as you get older to continue to work and how hard you want to work. Most of these long time route owners (or old timers) fall in a group I have mentioned earlier. The successful route owners who are honest, hard working, helpful, dedicated, sincere individuals who plan their work and work their plan day in and day out.

I am keeping my promise and trying my very best to give you a complete actual picture and a view of my experiences so you can make your own decision process in buying a route business and which route business easier and smarter. Just to remind you these old timers like my self all owned and operated Pepperidge Farm Cookies Route, some of them started with bread routes, potato chips, beverage and some were former supermarket employees. After number of years they realized that cookies routes are much easier to operate and takes less time to work then many other routes. They were also willing to pay so much more for a cookie route. Cookies and Crackers have approximately ninety days or more freshness date stamped on each package while bread has very short freshness date. Owning a bread route you have to go to warehouse every working day to pick up fresh bread. While most cookie routes owners go to warehouse once a week to load up. Cookie routes having ninety days or more freshness date stamped on each package all you have to do is a good job in rotating the product on the shelf to limit to very few out of date items. While bread being with very short selling dates, practically every time you go into the store you will have some items close to being out of sell by date that you must take out. Any bread route, brand name or any private label, be prepared to work harder and longer then a typical cookie route. The older route owners I mentioned earlier if they had a beverage or a juice route all those years do you really think most of them will be still working on their routes in their sixties. I don't think so.

For several years I worked for Pepsi Cola Bottling Of N.Y. as a district manager and I would go on the truck with different route owners to help them increase the sales and help to resolve any problems or situations they had. This way I had a first hand experience in learning how physically demanding that work really is when I helped them in putting the order together, deliver the order and packing it out. Not only is the product heavy, but also working outside the truck in rain, heat, and snow can be difficult. Even more challenging was when the company had a promotion for small convenience stores where they had to buy twenty five to fifty cases of soda to get five cases free or similar promotion. Storeowner would tell him to leave only few cases in the store to be packed out and the rest to put in his basement. The hand truck would be full of heavy soda going down steep basement stairs. Yes I did witness some injuries but mostly hard physical work by individuals who got used to the work. My point is for how long can you do this work and do it safely with out any injuries. Take your time in deciding which route to buy.

I AM NOT A SALESMAN OR A REPRESENTATIVE FOR ANY COMPANY NOR AM I ENDORSING ANY ONE COMPANY OR ANY ONE ROUTE TO BUY. MY OBJECTIVE, AND CONCERN IS FOR YOU READERS (THE POTENTIAL ROUTE OWNERS) TO COVER EVERYTHING THAT I POSSIBLY CAN ABOUT THE ROUTE BUSINESS SO YOU CAN UNDERSTAND IT, AS MUCH AS POSSIBLE AND THEN MAKE AN INFORMATIVE DECISION ABOUT PURCHASING THE ROUTE BUSINESS.

A brand name route is a protected route well established, offers a secure base, a predictable income, a known distributor and naturally a great benefit of nationally recognized successful name brand products. Just as important the ongoing support of the parent company in advertising, marketing, display fixtures, holiday displays and more important their area managers who's job is to help you grow the business and succeed. Another very important advantage of name brand routes is that all their route owners must use a hand held computer and generate an invoice for all the sales. Being a big chain store or a small local convenience store. This way when you are ready to invest your hard earned money into a route business you can be more assured that the sales figures route seller is giving you are same or very close to the figures you will get from the parent company for that route.

Route business is a very simple business once you learn it and you actually run it for several weeks and months. Just like any other business it does require a careful attention to detail. As I am writing this guide its September 2012 and the price of gas in N.Y.C. is approximately $4.30 a gallon. I don't think we will ever see a gallon of gasoline priced under

$3.00 a gallon. The reason I am writing about the price of gas is that it is a big part of your expenses in owning a route business. Another advantage of brand name route, which has a protected territory, is once you get to your route all your accounts are there. Over period of number of years owning and servicing this type of a route rather then one that has protected accounts that are scattered all over or an Independent Route difference in your expenditure on buying gas could add up to thousands and thousands of dollars.

Remember the saying (time is money) lets not forget the time you would spend traveling the distance from store to store if your route has no protected territory. It's not only the price of gas and your valuable time wasted, but also the wear and tear on your vehicle. As I mentioned earlier in this chapter the owners of Independent Routes can carry many different products from many different manufacturers and pick up the products from more than one wholesaler. In most cases there are no protected territories or protected accounts. Many different route owners could service the stores with same products. In this type of situations the store owner can demand lower price or extended credit, or possibly one of the route owners who is very aggressive in growing his business may offer one or both. Then there is always a chance in any one particular store that another route owner came before you to service the store and storeowner was sold out of that particular product and bought it from him.

There are some advantages of Independent Routes, the most important one is they are less expensive to purchase and you can sell the product anywhere you like. Remember my earlier saying "You get what you pay for "Most of independent routes don't use the hand held computer to generate a sales invoice. They can also buy from, different suppliers. How can you verify the sales figures 100% or close to it? With whom can you double-check the sales of each store for the last six to twelve months? If you cannot verify this to the point where you are truly and honestly comfortable with the sales figures the seller is giving you. How can you pay him the asking price? For that matter what is the fair price, something to think about and research very carefully? Keep in mind everything is negotiable.

Chapter 5
WHICH ROUTE TO BUY?

It's like asking what type of house to buy not an easy question to answer. I did mention earlier that I favor brand name route with protected territory and a predictable average weekly income. I don't mind paying the going market rate or established price in the route business for the route that I described and one that will give me the piece of mind and sense of security. For example if the route is averaging five thousand dollars a week in sales times thirty-six, the going price ratio in the market place. Price of the route would be one hundred and eighty thousand dollars. In most cases that include the truck, hand held computer and a printer.

As I am writing this, September 2012 in N.Y.C. area some routes are selling around the ratio of fifty- to one. Yes I agree with many of you, who think that is a lot of money. Pepperidge Farm Cookie Route that is averaging five thousand dollars a week in sales, an experienced route owner can correctly service it in two to three days. Working on twenty percent commission and minus the expenses, its still a very good financial reward for the time, effort and the flexibility it offers you of when to go to work and the time you want to go home. If you were selling bread on the route instead of cookies averaging the same weekly sales volume and earning the same commission and having same expenses it would be selling in N.Y.C. area approximately thirty -to one ratio. If you remember what I mentioned earlier bread routes require a lot more time and much more work. Every day you work you have to go to warehouse to pick up fresh bread and just about every store you service will have some items close to being out code of sell by date stamped on each item that you must take out give store credit and return it to the warehouse. This all takes time and effort. Some potatoes chips route go for fifteen-to twenty-to one ratio.

To answer the question on which route to buy it depends on you and your financial situation.
How old are you?
What physical condition are you in?
How hard are you willing to work?
How much money you need to make on weekly basis?
What is your marital status? Do you have a family to support?
How is your credit history?
These are some of the questions you have to think about and answer them. Be honest and realistic.
Hey? Its your money, invest it wisely.

Most brand name routes require you as the owner to operate the route. You will sign the distributorship agreement stating that fact. After number of years you have proven yourself as a very good route owner with an impeccable record to the company management and you wish to buy another route or add a second truck to your existing route you can hire a driver. You still have to manage your business.

Companies began selling routes to independent drivers, as route owners they have considerably more incentive to increase sales than an employee who is drawing a salary. Don't rush into any route business. By reading this book you already have taken the first important step, to learn all you can about the route business.
Make an appointment to see actual workings of a route business that you have interest in and the necessary capital to potentially buy it. Don't waste your time and the sellers looking at the route business that you know you don't have enough money for a down payment.
If you have limited capital to invest my advice is to look at the less expensive routes to buy, such as; bread, potatoes chips, pretzels, and others. Do your homework, research, talk to the route brokers, most of them are

very helpful and knowledgeable on many different route businesses. If you are totally set on purchasing more expensive route and you are short on the necessary funds for down payment, then simply wait so you can make and save the additional monies. Why go to a Mercedes Dealership if you only have the money and credit to qualify for a purchase of a Chevrolet.

Chapter 6

IS BUYING A ROUTE BUSINESS IN TOUGH ECONOMY A BAD DECISION?

In my 21 years of owning and operating a route business, I know that I probably experienced every economic cycle you can think of, so my answer is absolutely NO.

Most route businesses distribute and sell, name brand products, that have been successful sellers nationally, for years in the market place.

In a tough economy, owning a brand name route business has a big advantage, over many other small businesses. The parent company (the manufacturer of the products you are distributing,) may simply be more aggressive, in marketing, which can include; increasing the advertising on Regional or National Television, Radio, and Newspapers, Magazines, with discount coupon's inside. Also increase their promotional pricing in their major stores, etc.

You may have to work a little harder, every day to make up for a slow economy, like: offer the best possible service to all your accounts, put up as many promotional displays as you possibly can, in all the stores that is feasible, try to open and sell to any new accounts in your area etc.

OWNING A ROUTE BUSINESS, IT'S COMFORTING AND REASSURING TO KNOW, THAT YOU ARE IN THE BUSINESS FOR YOURSELF, BUT NOT, BY YOURSELF.

You have the power of a major brand. In most cases not only is the Corporation National, but International as well, behind you to help you succeed. In so many ways; like advertising, promotional pricing, many new and innovative products, special packaging, display racks, promotional material and so much more. They know that when you succeed, they will as well. It comes down to, team- work and partnership in growing the business, no matter what the state of the economy is.

Chapter 7

HOW MUCH CAN I EXPECT TO MAKE OWNING A ROUTE BUSINESS? IS IT A GOOD INVESTMENT?

Like any other business, the route business it depends on so many factors.
How big a route business do you plan to purchase?
It's weekly average sales?
Do you plan to work part time or full time?
How much money do you have to invest?
Do you plan to have any helpers?
What type of route business you are looking to purchase? Etc.

Most route businesses work on, approximately twenty percent profit margin, of their total weekly sales. If a route business you are buying is averaging for last six to twelve months eight thousand dollars a week in sales, your profit would be sixteen hundred dollars, minus your vehicle expenses such as; gas repairs, insurance, any warehouse fees, (some companies charge small weekly fees for receiving and storing the product), and use of any help. In my continued effort to help you get started in the route business, I would recommend you buy the business that you can operate on your own, learn the business totally, and understand all that route business requires. It may take you six to twelve months to fully learn all of you area, and the accounts you are servicing so you can build it, to its full potential. Then you have the experience, knowledge, and confidence in your self to decide if you like your route and the weekly income it generates.

Unless you have the previous experience in the route business and enough money to purchase a very large route then you might need a part time or full time helper. This is what makes a route business a perfect small business for owner operator, the flexibility it offers to purchase the size of the route you want, where you want it, and the opportunity to work hard and build its weekly sales and one day sell part of it for profit. You can also sell your name brand route business and buy the same type of route business similar in size just about anywhere in the country, should you or your family, ever have to move or simply chose one day to relocate.

To expand your route business?
Even after you did all you could to grow your existing route business you want and need to expand to make more money. You can sell you route when the opportunity comes to buy a larger route in the area you like, or possibly buy few accounts or a piece of territory from a fellow route owner who has too much to handle or simply wishes to work less, to downsize.

To downsize your route business, simply sell part of it.

Please don't start getting lazy and stop servicing all the stores on consistent basis as you have been doing or stop placing additional promotional displays. Not only are you hurting yourself financially on weekly earnings but also the value of your route business and the parent company's business at the same time. Very simply sell a piece of you route business territory, a few stores or certain amount of dollars in sales from your weekly volume. If that's not possible talk to your district sales manager and you fellow route owners to find out if they know of anybody who would be interested in buying a larger route and you purchasing a smaller one. Remember to try your very best to do the right thing by the parent company and their managers even if at times it might be very difficult to do. It will be in your best interest as time goes by and new opportunity comes up.

The reason I am saying this is when you wish to expand or downsize your business you need the approval of the parent company and their managers. Many times at the same time as you another route owner is looking to expand or downsize the business. The parent company and its management team always try their best to first help and accommodate the route owner who has proven himself over and over in increasing the sales and in trying his best to operate his business, as the parent company would like to. So try your best to be a professional and do the right thing every day.

How can you move your route business to another city or a state?

In most cases parent company has routes nationally. If you like to relocate or you must move, you let the company know well in advance, that you would like to move and sell your route business and buy one of similar size in the area you are moving to. You might wait six months or longer but is definitely possible. Several years ago a route owner of Pepperidge Farm Cookie and Cracker sold his route in N.Y.C. and at about the same time bought one in North Carolina with a weekly sales average very close to his route that he was selling. Here is another example where you need the help and the approval of the parent company and its management team. Always try to be a professional, honest, helpful, sincere, hard working route owner who is so dedicated as if the success of parent company solely depended on him. I think that not only will they help you with your plan but would go out of their way to do what ever they can to make it happen for you sooner rather than later.

Is route business a good investment?

In my many years of experience first as a district manager with Pepsi Cola Bottling Company of N.Y. and as a route owner with Pepperidge Farm I can honestly say its an excellent investment for owner operator. If you distribute a quality product with a nationally known company I feel is that much easier to get to "Your Route To Success." People have to eat and drink so why not buy a route business that sells one of the products that is proven to be a successful one nationally. Usually these types of routes cost more but in long term they are worth it. When your time comes to retire and sell the route business in most cases you will realize the substantial gain. Just about any route can be a profitable investment. In addition to earning a good living there are many other advantages;

1. This your business and you are working for yourself with the help and guidance from the parent company. Generally you set up you own schedule for the time you start working and the time you want to go home it gives you valuable freedom and the flexibility which most route owners take for granted.

2. All of your expenses associated with operating your route business are tax deductible. Vehicle expenses, parking tolls, repairs, depreciation, warehouse fees if any, hand held computer service contracts, telephone bills, and more. Also if you are paying off the promissory note to the seller of a route or any loan you took out to purchase the route interest you are paying can be written off as a business expense. As a self-employed individual, besides your regular yearly contribution to your I.R.A. you can also open a tax deductible S.E.P. I.R.A. Your own accountant can be of great assistance since keeping up with the latest tax laws is difficult, your focus is on increasing the sales and building an equity in your business. I opened my own S.E.P. I.R.A. long time ago, with the giant in the Mutual Fund Industry The Vanguard Group. The individual investors like you and me who invest in many of their Funds own them. This is the reason that they offer great service and advice at the lowest cost possible. I have been with them for a long time and they have always stressed the importance of diversification with all your investments and to always look at the long-term view on investing. Never try to time the market and buy and sell frequently as many of your brokers at times encourage you to do just that. My advice is to give them a call, and find out for yourself.

3. As you work hard and in time learn the route business you will increase the sales and the value of your route. Throughout the years in the business with good economy or bad, when fellow route owner wishes to sell the business or simply retire its fairly easy to sell the route business. Owning a route is not only a good investment but it comes with a tremendous advantage of job security, consistent income you can depend on, the flexibility of your own work schedule and the opportunity to expand your business, and make more money rather then waiting to get a raise, if you are lucky to get it on your job.

Your biggest challenge will be like it was for just about all route owners and me when you have limited capital, or only the minimum to put down to purchase the route business. Then your monthly note payment to the seller or the bank will be so large that it takes good portion of your profits. You like most of the route owners I met (including myself), you have to make the **NECESSARY SACRFICES FOR A BETTER TOMORROW**, for number of years to pay off the loan and build that route equity.

My fellow readers if success was easy, everybody would be successful. You have to look, at long-term picture, nothing worthwhile, is accomplished overnight. This is not a get quick rich business. I, and thousands of fellow route business owners, don't know any one of those types of businesses. The route business is getting rich slow, over period of time type of business.

The best scenario would be if you can pay for the whole route in full or at least try to put as much as you can towards the purchase price. Most quality brand name routes were you can make above average weekly take home earnings while working four to five days a week may cost three to four hundred thousand dollars. The more money you put down towards purchase price of the route the less your monthly payment will be on the loan. Borrow some money if you have to from your family, relatives or friends with a simple promissory note you can get notarized, or if lending party feels more comfortable go to an attorney. In case your potential lender has money siting in the bank at certain interest rate offer him more interest then the bank. Its not like you are going on a very expensive vacation or to a casino with the money explain to the lender your business plan and the money you will be making every week and how secure and steady the route business really is. Assure him he will get his money back at the agreed time. Not only will the person be earning more interest on his money but also the satisfaction of knowing he helped change your life for better and earning your gratitude and appreciation for his help in time of your need. In my experience of route ownership most of all route owners that I have met greatly benefited not only financially with route business ownership but also with overall quality of life. Most of the route owners

I met and many of whom I worked with were vibrant in good health and good physical condition. They liked the route business and the freedom and independence it gave them.

The amount of money you expect to earn on weekly basis depends on how big of the route are you purchasing. As I wrote earlier most brand name route owners work on average of twenty percent commission of their weekly sales. While owners of beverage routes make so many dollars per each case of product sold times the number of cases sold. Purchase price of route businesses and their profit margins do vary in different parts of the country, so when you are ready talk to your area route owners, call the route brokers, check the Internet etc.

More important question at this time then how much money can I expect to make owning and operating a route business is to ask your self: Do I like and am I going to like the route business five or ten years from now. Do I recognize and appreciate all the opportunities, the possibilities and all the advantages it has to offer comparing to working and making somebody else wealthy or working at the dead end job that you may hate and may not even have in the near future.

Just like any other investment you must view it as a long- term investment. Ask yourself were do you want to be and what do you want to do ten, fifteen or twenty years from now.

My advice to you is, don't buy any route business if you don't plan to own it and stay in the same route business for at least ten years. My advice comes from over twenty one years of experience owning and operating a route business and meeting and personally knowing so many successful route owners and just about all of them owned and worked their route businesses for ten to twenty years and more.

Simply put love what you do long enough and financial rewards will follow. When you love what you are doing it will not seem like you really are working.

In helping you decide on ownership of a route business, here are some additional questions to ask your self to further make your decision easier. Be honest with yourself, on your abilities, finances, and necessary sacrifices you and your family will have to make for a better more successful future.

The future that will be more predictable, with job and income security as the owner-operator of Route Business.

What made you look at the route business?
Why are you looking at this particular route business?
What are your financial goals for the next year? For the next five years?
What are you looking forward to most about owning a route business?
What is your ultimate business goal?
When do you want to retire?

You may have additional questions write them down.
Take your time in answering the questions honestly and realistically, it's all in your hands, in your control. I am just trying my best to help you.
They are all important questions to help you on;

YOUR ROUTE TO $UCCESS

Chapter 8
ADVANTAGES AND SOME CHALLENGES OF OWNING A ROUTE BUSINESS?

Like any other business, job or a professional career they all have their unique advantages and challenges. By now, you have learned of the many advantages of route business ownership that I have mentioned. As you finish reading this book you will learn and understand much more about the route business, that you can add your own personal advantages and challenges that you may have. Get a blank piece of paper and divide it in half and write it all down that specifically pertains to you and your present conditions, situations, and circumstances. This information will help you decide is the route business for you or not at this time in your life. At the time of writing this book the nationwide unemployment rate is well over 8% but at some big cities and states is well over 10%. The sad part is it has been over the 8% mark for last three years. Job or a career of route business ownership can not be outsourced or relocated abroad to far away places.

Advantages of owning a route business
You are your own boss
No retail store expenses

Service businesses are recession proof
Low overhead and start up costs
Flexible work schedule
Opportunity to expand your business
Many tax advantages of business ownership. Consult your tax advisor.
If you decide to buy a quality brand name route in most cases the parent company has a district sales manager to help you grow your business.
Part time or full time
No employees
Job security
Most routes have predictable secured income
Try your best to buy the route close to were you live to save time commuting plus money on gas and wear and tear on your vehicle. Owning a route you build equity with every payment you make towards your loan and every time you increase the sales.
Working on a regular job you are building equity and wealth for somebody else. Over time the appreciation you can expect, it should be clear that route ownership is as close to a financial no – brainer as you can get.
No franchise fees.
No royalty payments.

Challenges of owning a route business
Most good route businesses are expensive. You like most of the route owners must be willing to make necessary sacrifices for number of years until you pay off the loan. The weather conditions at times are not pleasant to work, in summer heat in N.Y.C. inside my step van it felt like an oven.
Every route has at least one very difficult person to do business with. You must have or develop discipline and patience to do business with such a person, because he or she may be the owner or the manager of one of your large accounts.

Its inevitable to leave some advantages and the challenges of route business ownership, so simply write them down, and all the questions that come up, while you are reading this book so you can get them answered at the later date.

You noticed the route business disadvantages I call them challenges, the reason being it's really how I personally feel about the route business in general. I don't see any disadvantages of owning a route business. There are some challenges that are not that difficult to overcome if you really love this business.

Chapter 9

WHERE CAN I BUY THE ROUTE BUSINESS?

I guess you already have decided that you would like to buy a route business since you came to this chapter. If my guess is correct, a big, congratulations. Its sad how many people don't know what they want, not to mention the young people in college who after three or four years are still not sure of what they want to do so they get an liberal arts degree with a very little chance of getting the job. For most route owners it was not an easy decision to make because there is a substantial investment involved. I must admit that because of my own experience, of owning a retail business prior to buying a route business, after only few hours on the route with a good friend I immediately decided to look to purchase a route business. It is a great feeling in deciding and knowing what you want. You also decide on what type of route, if not think about it and make decision. If you are not sure which type of route, why not look at two different ones and compare them, with their advantages and challenges and then decide. Keeping in mind the amount of money you have to invest, your overall financial situation and approximate dollar amount you have to have for a down payment.

Where can I buy the route, its almost like asking where can I buy the house.

You can call route brokers, look at the newspapers, Internet or call the companies directly. Maybe you have a friend in a route business or a friend of a friend who can introduce you to the route business. Also a relative or

38 | Where Can I Buy The Route Business?

a neighbor may work in the store were they are selling the products you thinking about buying a route that sells the same. That person can get you the name of route owner who delivers that product to the store. Once you have his name he can give you the name and telephone number of his area manager and additional information that you may need. You just never know, he may even know of a route for sale. All this takes time and patience. Many sellers list their route business exclusively with route brokers for certain period of time. They know that brokers pre- screen and pre-qualify the buyers so they don't have to be bothered with phone calls from people that in many cases don't have enough money for the down payment. Many of the potential byers don't do their homework in finding out the going price of the route in the industry they are interested so they spend time calling the sellers with out realizing they don't have the necessary funds.

Many name brand quality routes are sold on the inside or in the business through fellow route owners, who have a relative or a friend that is looking to buy the route or a parent company that already has a list of pre qualified candidates that want the route in certain price range or only in certain geographical area. If you do decide to fill out the application with a parent company so you can pre qualify to purchase a route, keep in mind the bigger you price range is, in buying the route business and more flexible you are, on the geographical area of your route to be located in, you greatly improve your chances of getting into the route business that much quicker. Do your homework, decide on the type of route business you want, its going price in the market place and the area or several areas you like for your route to be located in. Prices do fluctuate for same route businesses in different regions of the country and at times, from state to state and city to city.

Before you call the seller of the route and waste his time and yours, be at least somewhat knowledgeable and informative about that particular route business.

What is the going price of that route? Like most of the route owners when they started, if you don't have all the money to pay for the route, find out how much money you need to put down, to be able to get the financing. This is your business, your future, your hard earned money, your life work, time and effort we are talking about, don't rush into anything. When you find the right route business, you will know it. It will feel right, you will have a mind set as "Yes I can do this." You will feel good, positive and optimistic about the area were the route is located and the accounts that you will be servicing. You will believe in the product you will be selling and the parent company you will be representing in the market place as well as working with them very closely together as a team.

Just as important I believe is to have a trust and confidence in the route owner (the seller) that you are buying the route from and will spend number of weeks with him on the route learning everything that you possibly can about the route business. Especially his route, the area all the accounts and how he operates it. Its very important to carry with you pen and a notebook, and every day make notes on; how can you improve the route, store owners, and managers names, the receiving hours of the big chain stores, how many times a week does he service them, and on what days and so many other details. At the beginning it always seems difficult, and complicated, but its all repetitious so don't let it overwhelm you. Just in case the first several days working with the seller on the route your trust and confidence in him is not there and you feel that he is not being truthful on more than one occasion simply thank him and look for another route. In one of the chapters I mentioned if you don't plan on owning and operating a route business for at least ten years or more, then don't get involved. This is a business were you build equity and wealth over time not overnight.

My reason for writing this book is to help you decide on route business of your own, and to help you be successful in the business should you choose to buy one. Do your research in buying the route business directly from the route owner. Call the parent company they may have routes for sale, and don't forget the Route Brokers. Its a good idea to fill out the application with the parent company and pre -qualify, just as you would pre- qualify for mortgage loan when looking to purchase a house. The more money you have to buy or to put down towards a down payment along with a very good credit history and your flexibility on the area of the route to be located in, it will be easier and take less time to buy the route business you like. Remember what I wrote earlier that some route owners choose to sell their business exclusively through route brokers. God bless America, the land of the free, home of the brave, and freedom of choice. Why not both? Your own search, and stop by the route broker, (more then one) they have experience and knowledge in many different types of route businesses. Always carry with you pen and paper and write things down, ask questions, compile all the information so you can compare. What is best for you and your family? Look at the long-term picture, and write all the possibilities with owning a route business, along with some sacrifices you will have to make to reach your goals.

Ask yourself the following questions;

How much money will I be making two or three years from now?
Are there any opportunities to increase the sales on this route business I am purchasing?
Can I see my self-owning a route business ten years from now?
Add any other questions you may have, be objective, and realistic, while trying to cover all your bases.

IT'S YOUR MONEY INVEST IT WISELY.

To fill out the application with the parent company so you can pre-qualify, keep in mind the wider the price range in buying the route that you can afford, and you being more flexible, on the geographical area of the route to be located in, you will greatly improve your chances of getting into route business that much quicker. I remember with Pepperidge Farm for a period of time they had candidates for a route, already pre approved, and they were waiting for any routes that would come up for sale in Queens or Nassau County. While two routes were for sale in Manhattan (N.Y.C.), they did not want to deal with the cities traffic congestion, and the parking challenges, or they were possibly to lazy to get up at three in the morning like I did and many other route owners. These candidates to purchase the route in specific area, waited long time or simply gave up and moved on. I brought this up just so you are aware of it, and you can plan accordingly, and keep all your options open.

Chapter 10

RESPONSIBILITY OF A ROUTE OWNER.

1. Service

2. Selling

3. Inventory

1. Service

    Service all accounts in timely and orderly fashion.
    Establish service schedule and have one hundred percent compliance if for any reason you skip the stop make sure you service the stop the next day.
    Product is merchandised according to merchandising standards prescribed by the customer or a parent company. This usually pertains to large chain stores.

Display racks are placed in accounts on an as agree to basis.

    Try your best to place a display in high traffic location in the store. In many instances it is your relationship with store manager or an assistant that comes in very handy at this time. In time get to know them on first name basis and always try your best to do the right thing, like making sure your product section in the aisle is always well stocked

42 | Responsibility Of A Route Owner.

and the product is always fresh, no out of freshness code on any product on the shelf, and when your promotion is over, check with them about keeping up the promotional displays or not, after all they are the boss in the store. Whatever the answer they appreciate the fact that you asked them.

2. Selling

Fully develop and maximize all opportunities on a route.
Solicit every possible new account in the area of your route.
Try to sell a secondary location in accounts.
Use proper size promotional displays with price feature in high visibility locations.
If your promotional displays are empty on Monday morning, that means next time you should leave extra product in the back room or the basement to be packed out on Saturday or Sunday.
Always try to establish a good rapport with storeowners and all the managers.
Be a professional. (Try your best to be the best that you can be).

- Dress appropriately (like a salesman rather then a regular driver).

- To earn a respect you have to give a respect.

- Behavior is business like.

- Operate your route with honesty and integrity.

- Respect all store guidelines.

- Understand customer needs and complaints.

- Any conflicts, deal with it rationally, and ask for help and guidance from your area or district manager.

3. Inventory

- Rotate your product in all the accounts, on the truck and in the depot. First- in first- out.

- Avoid out of stock situations. (That's money out of your pocket and out of the storeowners).

- Always order extra product, especially the items that are on promotion. In case you do make a mistake of not ordering enough products, ask your warehouse manager, if any route owners have extra product that you can transfer from his inventory to yours. If still no luck have your area manager call another warehouse closest to you if anybody has extra items you need. Don't wait for the last day to take out stale or out of freshness code products from the store. You don't want customer to complain to the store manager.

Truck

- With out it you cannot go to work.

- Take care of it regularly. Keep it clean on the inside and on the outside.

- No visible damage on the truck.

- Remember your goal is to be a professional. Professional does not drive a dirty or damaged truck.

- Always drive safely and obey all traffic laws.

- Accidents and driving violations may not only hurt your pocket substantially on truck insurance, but you may get hurt and be out of business for a period of time and you may also injure somebody else, and possibly get sued.

Chapter 11
DO I NEED PRIOR ROUTE BUSINESS EXPERIENCE TO BE SUCCESSFUL?

The answer is no. Most of the route owners I met during my long period of time in the route business had no previous route business experience. Obviously any sales experience or previously working in the food industry is always helpful and advantageous. Most route businesses are simple and easy to learn. Some specialty routes may require some experience or more in-depth training. The seller will show you the route and teach you how he does it, as each route business has its own situations, needs, and circumstances. With the purchase of a brand name route many companies send their area manager with you first one to two weeks of owning a route to make sure you know the route and the correct way of servicing it. They will help, guide, teach, and inspire you in any way they can to increase the sales and make you and the company more successful. That is part of their job, so be smart, listen and work with them. Don't be afraid to ask for their help, assistance and advice whenever you feel that you need it.

By far, more important then having prior route business experience is you. Yes you? Your personality; your character, work habit, attitude, discipline, responsibility, reliability, confidence and desire to grow the business, and be successful. Do you really have what it takes to be successful in you undertakings? What is your work history, you credit history, marital status, financial situation, (your investments and total money you have to invest in the business). How much debt do you have?

What are your expenses? All companies with name brand routes want to know the answers to these questions. Naturally they approve the candidates who they think and have a feeling will help them grow their business, in the ever so very competitive market place. I personally knew off several candidates for purchase of a route business that did not get approved, even though they had more than enough money to put towards down payment of the route. I remember suggesting to them, to look at some Independent Route Businesses or to try to correct the situation or a problem that prevented them from getting approved to buy the brand name route business.

Name brand routes have been here for years, and will continue to be here for years to come, so you can try again to purchase one, when the right opportunity presents itself, and you took care of the problems that prevented you from getting approved the first time.

I devoted a whole chapter, (coming up) in covering just about all of the questions you might be asked, when you are ready to purchase a route business and all the information you have to have available.

Like I said earlier, most of the route businesses are simple and easy to learn and operate. However, I urge you to spend as much time as you can with the seller on the route to learn basically everything in how he runs his business. Then when you take over, you can improve on the things you saw, and have the confidence that you can do better and faster job then he did, to grow the business and make more money. THAT IS THE BOTTOM LINE, AN OPPORTUNITY TO EARN MORE MONEY.

Chapter 12

HOW MUCH MONEY DO I NEED TO BUY A ROUTE BUSINESS? WHAT IS THE BEST WAY TO FINANCE THE PURCHASE?

It's the same questions you would be asking if you were buying a house, it depends on how big, what type of route business, what area etc.

Have you decided on the type of route you want to purchase?

If you did, the next step is to find out the going price of the similar route in the type of route business you decided on. Talk to the sellers, brokers, and area managers anybody in the route business, look at newspaper ads, Internet ads and gather as much information as you can. After all; "It's your money, invest it wisely."

How much money do you need for a down payment?

How is your credit history, in order to qualify for the financing?

How much money do you need to earn every week, after all the expenses, to cover your living expenses, and any other debt payments?

As you can see its not an easy question to answer. Answer the questions above and write it down on paper, also write down all your financial information. You're savings, checking, all your investments like stocks, bonds, mutual funds etc. Write down the names of any relatives or friends (just in case) you may possibly have to borrow some money from. Since most of us don't have all the monies to pay for a brand name quality route business. You should try all the possibilities with having a goal in mind to put down as much as you possibly can to reduce the amount of the monthly note you will have to pay to the seller or the bank. You are looking to buy an established route business that is generating a weekly average of x – amount of money after all the expenses, this makes it much easier to work on your finances, any loans, and to figure out can you afford to purchase this particular route at this time or not. Remember that people will not stop eating or drinking any of the quality products sold by the route owners of nationally brand name route businesses. You are paying premium for a quality route business that you know it will be here ten or twenty and more years from now.

Don't be afraid to sell your investment holdings, or get a home equity loan that will be less expensive then the financing from the bank, or at times from the seller. Talk to your accountant and close relatives, and friends. Sit down and fully explain the route business, honestly and sincerely. You just never know who may help you financially or give you a valuable advice. If you are planning to borrow some money from relatives or friends, assure them, you like it done legally, through an attorney so they can feel protected and money will be returned with time frame and fair interest rate as agreed upon. Banks usually don't give out business loans to purchase a route business, in case of default; they are not going to take back the route. Just as all types of route businesses are priced differently they also have different financing arrangements.

As of this writing with Pepperidge Farm Routes either bread or cookies and crackers you need at least twenty percent of the sale price of the route as down payment, and a very good credit. Then you can finance the rest, through the bank that Pepperidge Farm is working with (basically guaranteeing the repayment of the loan). The more you put down and being debt free with excellent credit history, will greatly improve your chances of getting approved to buy the route. They will look very closely at your assets and debts and monthly living expenses as well as any other sources of income, as well as the projected weekly income from the route and future monthly note payments. They will compare it all to see if its workable and in the best interest of both parties. They want to protect themselves and you. Why approve you for the purchase and the financing if your monthly living expenses and future monthly note payments are almost as large or larger then the income from the route, and your other sources of income. In case you are very close financially, or in this type of scenario, and you really like the route, the product line and the parent company, don't give up. Write down all your options; borrowing from your family, relatives or friends, buying a smaller route, if it's a four day route, maybe working another job, part time for a period of time. In one of the chapters I mentioned that many brand name route owners started with a less expensive routes, such as bread, potatoes chips, pretzels and more. They generally make the same percentage in commission; the difference is that they usually work harder, and longer hours to earn the same money on weekly basis.

Don't forget to look at the long picture of the route ownership, that once you pay off your name brand route; you will have the steady secured income, job security, a recession proof business, low expenses, flexible schedule, ability to expand you business, or sell part of it to have more time for all your leisure activities. How many people can say that about their job, business or any profession? Remember to stay in touch with route brokers who may have exclusive listing of a route seller who may be willing to carry the note with the requirement of higher percentage of the sale price as a down payment. Do all your homework, research, ask questions, investigate, but do it honestly and sincerely don't waste peoples time or make promises you can not keep.

(In the next chapter I will discuss; "Ways to save for a down payment on a route business). I must say it's a must read if you want save money for anything you wish to have.

Keep in mind that with many other small businesses, you may need employees, store, office or a warehouse, and so many other expenses that you do not have with owning a route business. Something to think about before you invest in any other small business.

It's a tough time to be an investor. Volatile markets and banks offering very little interest on your hard earned money. Investors have genuine concerns and the past decades volatility has scared young people in particular away from stocks. According to an October 2011 article in Forbes, forty percent of investors in "Generation Y "– between ages eighteen and thirty agree with the statement. "I will never feel comfortable investing in the stock market."

Owning and operating a route business for a long-term success has not changed in decades. People will not stop eating or drinking the products route owners are delivering every single day.

On your route to success in trying to achieve financial security and saving for retirement; its better to focus on the investment you can control. Investment like owning a route business or rental property will let you decide- when to start to save and how much to save. Because that's, THE MOST REALIABLE WAY TO SUCCEED IN MEETING YOUR GOALS, IS WHEN YOU ARE IN CONTROL.

Chapter 13
WAYS TO SAVE FOR DOWN PAYMENT ON THE ROUTE BUSINESS, OR FOR ANY OTHER INVESTMENT, OR A BIG -TICKET PURCHASE.

One of the most important features of route ownership and it's the one thing about, that is most responsible for making route owners well off financially, and that is owning a route turns you into a "saver."

Why is this so important?

It's very simple.

People who have money have it because they saved it. People who don't didn't. Route business ownership creates savers. Each time you make a payment towards your loan you took out to purchase a route business, you're saving money. That's because with each payment you're reducing your loan balance and that in turn is building you equity. For most route purchases you need to have twenty to thirty percent of the purchase price, as a down payment, with a very good credit. If you really like to own a route business and you know you don't have enough for a down payment, here is a sure way to save the money you need.

Open up your "Route Savings Account"

Go down to your local bank and open a savings account. Tell the bank you're not interested in an account that comes with an ATM card or checking privileges (reason being you don't want to be tempted to spend any of the money you put into it). Rather you're looking for an account that offers the highest interest rate available. In order for a savings plan to be effective, "The process has to be automatic." You need to have a system that doesn't depend on you having to do anything, except going to work. This means setting up a regular payroll deduction or checking transfer that automatically move a specified amount of money to your "Route Savings Account,' on a specific day of the month. This is the surest way for you to save the necessary money you need for a down payment on the route business. We all know that sticking to a savings plan for a period of time is as hard as sticking to a diet plan, or maybe harder for most people. We live in a consumer oriented society that's constantly tempting and urging us to spend and buy rather then save for a better tomorrow. Have your paycheck deposited automatically in you bank account. It will save you both time and money. Using direct deposit allows you to know exactly when your paycheck will be in your checking account; you can now pick a specific day of the month for a specific amount of money to be automatically transferred from your checking account to your "Route Savings Account." Just about every bank offers this service it is automatic funds transfer or systematic savings. [2] It really works, just do it, if you really have a deep belief and desire that owning a route business is truly;" **YOUR ROUTE TO SUCCESS."**

How much should you save?

Obviously that depends on your particular circumstances. How much money you already have and the price of the route. Keep in mind the more you put down towards the purchase of the route the less your monthly payment will be on the loan. Then again if it's a good size route were your earnings will cover the monthly payments and your other expenses then get to buying that route business as quickly as you can. Your top financial

---

2 Automatic Millionaire Homeowner by David Bach

priority should be saving the money you'll need to become a route owner, a businessman, being your own boss on the road to financial independence.

To speed up the process to route ownership consider in making a radical change in your lifestyle?

Make a radical change in your life style is much easier said then done. What keeps many people from owning a route business or for that matter any business, is that they're not willing to change their current life style, or make the necessary sacrifices in order to get what they really want. Most people simply live beyond their means, they buy or lease luxury cars, wear designer clothes, often eat out in pricy restaurants, yet they complain that they are living from paycheck to paycheck, they cant save any money. If your desire is strong, deep and a burning desire and is what you think about most to get what you really want (route business, a better home what ever it may be) you must and will find the courage and discipline to make positive changes in your life. Drive a less expensive car, buy fewer clothes, eat out less, cut back on entertainment expenses, rent a smaller apartment or live in a less expensive neighborhood and so on. For a really big change in your lifestyle to save the most money consider moving in with your parents, relatives, or your in laws if they have the room and are willing to help you for a period of time.

ASK YOURSELF?

What kind of lifestyle change, could you make right now, to have the future you want?
It's having a vision that's clear, realistic, and feels just right for you, not to impress your friends and neighbors. If you don't have a life you really want, you have to accept the fact that just buying, accumulating stuff, and spending your money will not change it for better until you start asking questions, when is enough. You have to stay focused on what is important, real, fair, responsible, honest, and what decisions, choices, and actions you take are going to help you get to were you want to be, and what you want to accomplish.

Think about it very carefully and write it down, every possibility that you can think off, every person that could help you get to; "YOUR ROUTE TO SUCCESS."

Living smart, efficient, and below your means is always better the living large ahead of yourself.

Here is another idea that will begin to transform your financial situation immediately. Every time you spend any money for anything.

ASK YOURSELF THIS QUESTION:

"Is this purchase really necessary and will it really bring me closer to financial security or help me realize my financial goals?"

This will help you develop, money consciousness's, and the drive, to reach financial goal you may have in mind. It forces you to act responsibly and with discipline. Asking the money question will make you visualize or consider what goals are most important to you several times a day, every time you spend a dollar or make a purchase of any kind. It automatically keeps you awake and alert as to what your life goals are all about. It keeps you from drifting off into idle day – dreams and wasting your time and your money. This technique will keep your drives and ambitions alive and in your consciousness at all times.

You can extend this idea to everything you do, how you spend your time, what kind of entertainment or recreation you engage in etc.

You could ask something like this:

"Is this the best way to spend my time now, is it really necessary, or could I do better spend this time doing something more important that will help me achieve my financial and personal goals in life?"

"Or is this really the best action for my ultimate mental, physical and financial well being?"

For example should you spend two to six hours or more watching T.V. or be on the internet, or could that time be better spent reading a book that would help you in your business or any other goals in life. By asking yourself these questions it will force you to keep in mind at all times what is important to you in life, what are your priorities, how can you best use your time, money and resources to accomplish your goals. It helps you discipline yourself, to channel your time, your thoughts and your energies it the right direction.

TO TAKE THIS EVEN FURTHER, ASK YOURSELF;

How much money did you spend on entertainment last month?

Sporting events, concerts, cable or satellite T. V., Broadway shows, **movies** and so on.

Write it all down and add it up. Be honest with yourself or don't bother.

Then write down how much did you spend last month on self- improvement, to achieve the success and financial independence you want. Did you buy any self-improvement books, disks, or attended any seminars and so on. We all know the answer, what we don't know is how much the disparity between the two is. Only you know how great the disparity is between the two behaviors are.

My fellow readers if people spend just the tiny fraction of the money they spend on entertainment on the self-improvement instead. Our country's budget would have a surplus rather then a deficit. A deficit so large that is not only threatening the American Dream for so many, but also our very way of life. Then there will be a very little need for any of the subsidized programs that sadly to many of our fellow citizens rely on every day and the numbers are growing.

Majority of us would be health conscious, how physically fit we are, disciplined on the way we spend and manage our money, wiser on how we use our credit and credit cards in particular. We would learn to be self-reliant and work to be able to afford to buy only the things we need and can afford rather then buying the things we want and can not afford to buy.

Years ago I started asking myself these type of questions and slowly my overall quality of life improved. For example I used to watch just about all major sporting events on television, for many years sitting on the couch watching the millionaires play, who appeared to have more fun then me, while I was just sitting there watching the world go by. So I stopped watching, I got up from the couch and started going to the park, playing tennis, walking, running. I decided to go back to the library again and getting self-improvement books, and books on being a better and more successful small rental property owner. After a while not only did I feel better physically but also emotionally in overall better state of mind then before. I felt like I was doing and accomplishing something rather then sitting and watching television.

Here I am, just retired, and writing a book of my successful business experiences, trying to help everybody out there who wants to change his or her life for better and to find that elusive;" Joyful contentment in life." Reaching a point in your life of having enough.

My goal is to wish and hope is to help you find it, and to truly make a positive difference in your life.

Too many people spend money they haven't earned, to buy things they don't want, to impress people they don't like.

Will Rogers
American actor, humorist and writer

Chapter 14

IN THE EVENT I GET SICK OR I WANT TO GO ON VACATION, WHO WILL TAKE CARE OF MY ROUTE BUSINESS?

It all depends on the type and size of the route business. Don't be overly concerned. Each route owner, and every company have their own plans and procedures for such circumstances. When you go on the route that you are looking to purchase that is one of many questions you will be asking the owner. When I worked for Pepsi Cola Bottling of N.Y. as district manager most of the route owners had helpers who were capable of operating the route. As the route owner with Pepperidge Farm very few distributors had helpers. If I got sick for a day or two nobody would service the route. The first day back naturally I would service my key accounts first. Your area manager, storeowner or store manager nobody likes to see your shelves' empty, and you simply work longer and quicker for few days until you all caught up. A responsible, caring, professional route owner will have contact telephone numbers for all his accounts and will communicate with them to let them know the reason why is he late in servicing their stores. In case you are sick for more then three days let your area manager know. Then you can have any route owner service the larger accounts that you know will need service or your area manager will ask the distributor who's area or accounts are closest to you to service them. Route owners who service your stores will use their truck and inventory and get the commission.

The area manager has to put your accounts that need service (while you are sick or on vacation) into the hand held computer of a route owner that will service them. As all major companies require that all sales must be done through the hand held computer. No hands written bills are allowed. Smaller independent routes have no hand held computer so the bills are hand written.

As far as your smaller accounts, you know them best, for how long can you not service them before the shelves get totally empty. You can have more the one route owner covering your accounts while you are sick. You should take a vacation during your slowest time of the year, for me with selling cookies and crackers the slowest time was, right after Christmas and the week of Fourth of July. The idea is to plan your vacation well ahead and coordinate with your fellow distributors who are closest to your accounts so you don't plan to go on a vacation at the same time. You cover for each other, and give him a list of accounts that need to be serviced and special circumstances for certain stores, as far as the time receiving opens and closes, do you have any secondary or promotional displays in the store, and their location and so on. If any special promotion is going on in any of your stores so the fellow distributor can order extra product that is on sale. Distributor will service the accounts you give him with his truck, his inventory so naturally he will get the full commission. Most route owners I met, financed their route businesses by putting twenty to fifty percent of the purchase price as a down payment. So most, including myself did not take a week long vacation until we paid off our loans, which took five to ten years. Majority of us would simply take many three-day weekends off at the slowest time of the year. Remember it's your business, your success depends on the time and effort and necessary sacrifices you choose to make. You don't work and sell, you don't get paid.

It's nice to have a choice or be in control of what, you want to do.

Another great thing of route ownership is being your own boss, in control and knowing harder you work the more money you will make. Working for somebody else is like going to the gym for five days and your boss is the one with the muscles.

Chapter 15

DO MOST ROUTES INCLUDE THE VEHICLE? WHERE DO I KEEP THE VEHICLE? DO I NEED A SPECIAL LICENSE TO DRIVE?

Do most route businesses include the vehicle?

Just about all route business purchases include the truck or a step van. Unless you are buying a route from a seller who's route has grown so much that he can no longer handle it with one vehicle and instead of buying another vehicle and hiring a driver he decided to sell part of his route. Then in this type of case you should expect to pay less for the route business, and buy your own vehicle. Before closing on the route business check the vehicle and have your mechanic inspect it and find out; When was the last oil change, tune up, how is the wear on the tires. Uneven wear on front tires usually vehicle needs a wheel alignment or front end work. Your mechanic will check for many other potential problems or safety issues. If some repairs are necessary negotiate with the seller either to fix and pay for the repairs or deduct it from the selling price.

Where do I keep the vehicle?

That is also one of the many questions that you will be asking the seller when you are on a route with him to see the business. Here in N.Y.C. most of my fellow route owners kept their Step Vans or small Box Trucks in commercial truck parking lots or gas stations that have the extra space. They paid approximately two to three hundred dollars per month. Outside of N.Y.C. or any other big city where the parent company has extra parking space next to their plant or a warehouse free parking is provided. It also depends on the type of route. Routes selling bread, cookies, potatoes chips, pretzels, route owners load their own truck with product. With route such as Pepsi Route were the parent companies employees load the trucks during the night the trucks must be parked by the warehouse to be loaded with product. Keep in mind that it also depends on how far you live from your warehouse were you pick up the product and the area or the location of your major accounts in deciding where is the most convenient area to park your vehicle. Just as important is in knowing how many times a week do you have to go to a warehouse to pick up product. When you are on the route with the seller make a note of all of this to see how far from your house is your protected territory or protected accounts route, where is the warehouse located that you will be picking the product from.

I keep repeating the following statement because it might save you a lot of time, money and many headaches. "Don't buy a route business if you don't plan to own and operate it for ten years and more." Very simply try your best to buy the route, as close to were you live as you can. I know of several route owners who lived in the area of their own route's protected territory. How much time and money did these owners saved over ten or more years, in savings on gasoline alone could be in thousands of dollars, not to mention the wear and tear on their vehicles, as well as the convenience to come home for lunch if you like. In my own case when I started there was no Pepperidge Farm Route for sale close to were I lived so I bought one in Manhattan (N.Y.C.) about thirty minute drive.

Chapter 15

Do I need a special license to drive?

For most route businesses all you need is a regular drivers license. You will be driving a step van or a small box truck, that come in different length sizes and also the height and width. Beverage route businesses usually need a C D L license. The seller will give you all the information about the license issue. More important then the need for a special license is having a clean driving record for at least last five years. If that's not the case do all you can to try to correct the problem in any way possible, so the parent company does not hold back, your approval for the purchase of the route. Also to avoid the insurance company from charging you so much more for the coverage or even trouble getting the insurance since they will know you will be diving a lot by owning a route business.

Chapter 16

MONEY SAVING TIPS ON VEHICLE INSURANCE.

Just about all-successful route owners that I have met, while working at Pepsi Cola as a district manager or as a route owner, practiced being frugal. That means you do the necessary homework to do comparison-shopping for your vehicle insurance if not every year at least every two years. The rates substantially do vary from year to year and company to company. With commercial vehicle insurance you do have a much smaller pool of insurance companies to pick from but try your best to compare with several companies. Check if you can take advantage of any group rates offered by professional, business and trade association. Try to buy all your insurance needs from the same insurer to see if that will save you any money. To get the best rate I always took the highest deductible the insurance company offered.

Route business requires you to drive a lot more then most other small businesses. It's very important to pay close attention in how you drive your commercial and private vehicle. Your goal is to have a clean driving record. Insurance companies know you are driving for a living and will pay close attention to your driving record. In case you choose to buy a small route, working only three or four days and driving much less the twelve thousand miles a year, which is a typical yearly average for most drivers, make sure to tell this to your insurance company to see if you can get some discount on your policy.

Money Saving Tips On Vehicle Insurance.

Even if you have a perfect driving record don't forget to take the Defensive Driving Course every three years. You will automatically get a ten percent off on liability part of the insurance on all the vehicles registered to you. That is substantial savings over number of years you will own a route business and savings while you continue driving your car when you retire. Just as important is that the course itself will remind you of things we don't think about or pay attention to, in helping you to be a better defensive driver. The cost of the course is about forty, to fifty dollars. Ask your local driving school when do they offer the course, it lasts about five hours. I can tell you from my long experience that is well worth the time and effort. Even though I am retired I still take the course every three years, not only to save money, but also to be a better driver.

Chapter 17
THE QUESTIONS YOU MUST HAVE ANSWERS TO, BEFORE YOU ACTUALLY START LOOKING TO BUY A ROUTE BUSINESS.

I am trying my best, to make a process of buying a route business easier for you, so don't waste time, and call the sellers or brokers if you are not ready yet.

1. Have you definitely decided on what type of route business you like to purchase.
Yes or No
You can look at two or three routes, meaning that you would be selling different products. Being flexible this gives you a greater opportunity of buying a route closest to your home, or the area you prefer, the size of the route, and most important this way you can buy the route business for the amount of money that you have to invest. Being flexible on which route to buy gives you room to negotiate the price and terms of the sale.
2. How big a route can you afford to buy?
How many days are you planning to work?
Do you plan on having a helper?

3. Write down all the funds you have available to invest, savings, checking, all the investments, possibility of home equity loan, seller financing, or borrowing from family and relatives.
Once you have the answers for the above questions and you found a route you like to purchase. The next step is.
4. Is the seller asking price the going rate in the market?
5. How is his price compared to other similar routes or most recent routes sold?
Talk to the seller's area manager and the brokers you have contacted earlier for their suggestions and input.

This is a major decision, your business, your career a way to provide for you and your family. It should be a family decision. It is a joint venture that will have the impact on the entire families, time, money, and a way of life. Keep in mind once you find the route that you really like, feel good about, and the seller is a good person who takes his time to show you and tech you the business. Do all your homework quickly, and stay in contact with the seller and his area manager as other potential buyers maybe looking to purchase it also. Do not loose out, on a purchase of a very good route, for a difference of a few thousand dollars.

Example; you finally found the route you really like. I mean the route of your dreams. The final price is three hundred thousand dollars. The seller already came down from the asking price of three hundred and twenty thousand dollars. You are willing to pay him two hundred and ninety thousand dollars. If you are positive and certain that you like the route, and you plan to own and operate it for at least ten years or more. If that is the case then write down the dollar amount being ten thousand dollars difference between your offer and the final asking price of the seller and divide it by the amount of days in ten years.

Then decide is it worth loosing this route, this opportunity that you are certain is right for you all for few additional dollars a day during the ten year period, if you own the route for longer then that, then it comes even less, maybe down to the price of cup of coffee. There is no perfect route business or any other business or a job that is perfect.

I feel that route business gives you more control, flexibility, more freedom, opportunity for financial independence and self-reliance, things that you simply can't get with a regular job. Every route has its advantages and challenges. My advice is to spend as much time as you can in the area and in the accounts you are planning to purchase. Always carry with you pen and a note pad and write things down, like potential new accounts, gaining more selling space, placing display racks and so on. After spending one or two weeks with the seller on the route and visiting the area on your own, summarize all the advantages and challenges of this particular route. If after careful and thorough review of the results, price of the route, your weekly earnings and expenses and your potential for growth, you are not excited about the opportunity but rather not sure and doubtful simply walk away and look for another route. Don't forget to thank the seller, area manager or a broker for their time, and be honest with them on your decision. Explain to them the reasons for your decision, you never know, the seller may come down on price if that is the major sticking point. Nobody likes to feel like they were used. You may also have some additional questions at later date that they can help you answer it. My advice is don't burn any bridges behind you.

Chapter 18

IF YOU REALLY WANT TO BUY A ROUTE BUSINESS AND TRULY BELIEVE IN, "YOUR ROUTE TO SUCCESS "(OR ANY OTHER SMALL BUSINESS).

Then make a promise, and commitment, to yourself and the dead line for its achievement.

I _____ am confident that I can succeed in owning a route business.
   Name

I promise myself that I will start looking at possibility of owning a route business or any other small business; by _____
                     Date

I will make an offer on a route business (any other small business) by no later then. _____
      Date

I promise my self that I will own a small business by _____
Date

Many people will read this and won't do anything.
Some will take action.
Join them.
Let others wish, hope, and dream by buying a lottery ticket.
Don't wait until all your conditions are right to start.
You might wait rest of your life.
There is no perfect time for success.
You have the desire, motivation, and a can do attitude to work and courage to take the next step.
You promised and made a commitment to yourself.
If you can't be true to yourself, you can't be true to anyone. There are lots of aspects of our lives we don't have control over, but we do have control of ourselves.

JUST GO AND MAKE IT HAPPEN.

None of us can change our yesterdays,
But all of us can change our tomorrows

Colin Powel
Secretary of the United States under President George W. Bush

Chapter 19

SAMPLE QUESTIONS AND PERSONAL INFORMATION YOU MAY BE ASKED WHEN YOU ARE READY TO PURCHASE.

(This is only to help you gather and prepare your personal information. Some companies may not be asking this many questions.)

Name:	Social Security #:
Driver's License #:	
Home Address:	
City, State, Zip:	
Phone # (Home, Business, Cell):	

| Date of Birth: | Height: | Weight: |

How long have you lived at present address?:

What was your previous address?:

| Marital Status: | Number of Children: |

How many people depend on your financial support?:

Spouse's Occupation:

How many years of formal education?:

Did you graduate high school?:

| What was your class standing?: | Upper Half | Lower Half |

Any specialized training (describe briefly):

Favorite subject in school:

What publications do you read?:

To what groups or organization do you belong?:
What sports or activities do you participate in?:
Have you been involved in any traffic accidents during the past five years?:
If yes, please describe:
Have you been arrested or fined for traffic violations within the past five years?:
If yes, what were the reasons?:
Have you ever been convicted of or plead guilty or no contest to anything other than traffic violations?:
If yes, please describe:
Military Service: Yes ( ) No ( )
Dates: From   to   Branch:

Your Route to Success | 71

| Rank: | Type of Discharge: |

| Work History |

| Present Business or Employer: |

| Address: |

| City, State, Zip: |

| Starting and Ending Net Income: |

| Reason for change: |

| Immediate supervisor's name: |

| In how many companies did you have sales experience? |

| Which of your jobs proved to be the most interesting? |

| If you were not entirely successful at some job, what was the cause? |

| What do you feel is your greatest business assets? |

What kind of work are you very good at?
Have you ever had two jobs at the same time?
What are the things about (this company or route) that appeal to you?
Why does becoming a distributor of (this company or route) appeal to you?
What net income (before taxes) do you expect from your route after 5 years? 10 years?
How do you feel about taking care of your business during odd hours, such as early mornings, nights, or weekends?
What would you like to be doing ten years from now?
Financial History

What sources of income do you have outside of your job?
How much outside income do you receive per month?
How much does your spouse earn?
If you own a home, what are your monthly payments?
If you rent, how much is your rent per month?
What is your minimum monthly cost of living (including food, utilities, insurance, etc.)?
Have you been bonded?
Name and Address of your bank:
Branch office used (if more than one list separately):

Present fair market value of your home:
Amount of fire insurance on your home:
Original amount of your mortgage:
Amount of your mortgage paid off:
Amount of balance owed on your mortgage:
Name and Address of Mortgage Holder:
Credit and Character Reference:
List the places where you now have credit:
Store, Company, or Credit Card Name:
Address:

Store, Company, or Credit Card Name:
Address:
Character Reference Name: Phone #:
Address:
Relationship:
Character Reference Name: Phone #:
Address:
Relationship:
Assets and Liabilities

Assets (List only assets that are in your name and/or spouse's)
CASH:
Checking accounts:
Savings accounts:
Certificate of deposits:
IRA/KEOGH:
Life insurance (cash value only):
Stocks and Bonds:
Other securities:
Subtotal cash:
Personal Property (List fair market value):
Home (Residence):
Vehicles:
Tools:

Equipment:
Boats and Trailers:
Subtotal of personal property:
Other Assets (List fair market value):
Real Estate:
Misc. Items:
Subtotal of other assets:
Total Assets:
Liabilities

Mortgage or Loan Balance:
Home (residence):
Other real estate:
Vehicles:
Boats:
Charge Accounts (itemize):
Subtotal of charge accounts:
Other
Personal Loans:
Judgments:
Liens:

Other Debt:
Subtotal other:
Total Assets:
- Total Liabilities:
Net Worth:

Chapter 20
HOW TO INCREASE YOUR WEEKLY SALES AND IN TURN EARN MORE MONEY AND VALUE OF YOUR ROUTE BUSINESS?

To increase the sales on your route or very simply to really succeed in the route business beyond your expectations.

YOU MUST BE FLEXIBLE, ADAPTABLE, AND WILLING TO CHANGE, MAKE ADJUSTMENTS, WITHOUT BEING AFRAID OF HARD WORK SWEAT AND NECESSARY SACRIFICES FOR THE LONG- TERM SUCCESS. THIS IS ONE OF MY SECRETS IN OWNING A ROUTE BUSINESS. READ IT OVER AND REALLY UNDERSTAND IT. ONCE YOU DO, PUT IT TO USE AT WHAT EVER YOU DO. KNOWING IS NOT ENOUGH WE MUST APPLY AND DO.

When I bought my Route Business I immediately increased the weekly sales volume. I copied everything positive the previous route owner was doing on the route, and then I build on that foundation, on that base that he established. The very first thing I did was increase in the service frequency to my largest stores on the route. Some stores that he serviced once a week I started servicing twice a week. The even larger stores that he serviced twice a week I started servicing three times a week. Storeowners and managers absolutely can't stand seeing empty shelves or close to being empty. Not only do they loose the sales but also have unhappy customers, and if the product is on a promotion many stores give rain check slips (which means customer can get the product on sale price after the end of a promotion. Also if storeowner or store managers notice your promotional cardboard display empty they will simply take it away and discard it. Further you may not get the permission to replace the promotional display.

The increase in service frequency to your key accounts is the single most important step that you can take to increase the sales on your route. With increase in service frequency to your key accounts not only do you increase the sales, but also you build a rapport with storeowner, manager, and a whole management team. By you providing an excellent service to their store they know that they can count on you to help them in increasing their own stores sales, and keeping the customers happy by eliminating out of stock conditions, by always having enough product that's on special promotion and your product always being fresh. Also your shelve space in the isle always being well stocked and maintained in clean condition. Simply put it's a win –win situation for all concerned, you, the company you represent, the store, and the stores customers. As well as your area manager, and the whole management team, of the parent company, being pleased with your increase in sales and service.

In time you will get to know store owners, managers on the first name basis, their interests, hobbies and so on, you will build trust, reliability, honesty, integrity, and maybe a friendships. This is so important in time when you are looking to get a secondary permanent display for new products or your best selling items. Also when the time comes to ask for a best possible location in the store for your promotional product display. When your products are on sale, if your promotional display is located in front of the store by the check out lines, you may sell hundreds or even thousands of dollars worth of product more, then if the location of the display was in back of the store, in the corner someplace where very few customers see it.

Chapter 20

Depending on the size of the store you can have one, two, three or more promotional displays all over the store. Now you can see the critical importance not only of your service frequency but your overall personality, work habit, reliability, honesty, integrity, conduct, and your personal appearance.

Is your personal appearance and your dress code closer to resembling a salesman, business owner or closer to resembling a truck driver. At the end of the day, and your long-term success it matters a great deal? I am writing from experience, many times on the route many new managers thought that I was a district manager because of my appearance, but on few occasions I was in an awkward situation were I could've dressed better. I also met some route owners that simply looked more like homeless on the street, rather then a business owner, if I was the storeowner I would have to think twice for letting them in my store, let alone do business with them. I am not telling you to wear a suit and a tie on a route, simply to dress well, casual, look clean and respectable, act and feel successful. Show the pride and enthusiasm in who you are, the company you represent and the quality products you are selling.

Next step in increasing your sales, as I just mention is to be sure to place promotional displays in all the stores were the sales promotion is going on. Try your best to secure the placements of promotional displays in the best possible location in the store. Depending on the size of the store and your personal relationship with an owner or a manager try asking for more than one display. If not successful ask for an extra display just for the weekend when the store is most active. In many cases I would place an additional display on Friday and take it down while servicing the store on Monday. On my Queens Route, I had two supermarkets close to one another that were a part of large chain of stores. Both stores were small, but very busy and at times I had a tough time getting permission to place one display up let alone another one for the weekend. This is one of many advantages in your route being close to your residence. In one of the earlier chapters I mentioned to try to buy the route close to were you live. You save not only on traveling time to and from work but the wear and tear on your truck. As I am writing its October 2012 and the price of gas in Queens is 4.15 a gallon. Since I lived close to these stores I would ask the store manager could I leave some extra product in the stores storage area with my Friday's delivery. I would go on Saturdays before they close or Sunday morning soon as they opened to pack out the extra product I left. Route owners that service Wal-Mart's or Targets that always have some kind of a special promotion going on, do this every weekend or they pay someone to pack out for them.

Once you did all you can in you larger accounts to secure the placement of promotional display and you had no success in one or two stores don't be afraid or reluctant to ask your area manager for help. That is part of their job, to help you sell more products and succeed. In many instances they are successful, because of many years of experience in handling similar problems, situations and circumstances that many route owners face.

Opening new accounts is another sure way to increase the sales.

Only after you are completely sure that all your accounts are being serviced correctly do you try to open new accounts. Just about every route has some new accounts to be opened and serviced. When I started on my route, the previous owner had large area to cover with to many stores to be serviced and with just one truck he could not service it all, so he chose not to buy the second truck and to expand his business, but instead, to sell me part of the route with protected territory. Route owner made a profit from the sale of part of his route and now created more time for himself to concentrate on growing the sales in his other accounts, as well as time to open smaller stores that he previously had no time to service. My route was located in down town Manhattan (N.Y.C.) near Wall St. area, with many office buildings having news stand in their lobby. They were all small accounts that previous owner had no time to service. I had to park my step van close to most of the newsstands to service my other accounts so it was a no brainer to try to service them. Within several months I opened approximately thirty newsstands with each averaging about fifty dollars a week in sales (this was twenty one years ago) that was a nice weekly sales increase. I did not open every new account that I visited. I tried my very best, but some storeowners did not want to sell the product. I did not give up easily I asked my area manager for help, explaining fully the situation and objections so together we can plan on the strategy of convincing the owner to try to sell our product.

As I mentioned I had a protected territory type of a route so my plan as well as my goal was to know and learn of every potential new account in my area. I drove and walked through every block on my route, discovering many potential new accounts such as; schools, hospital gift shops, catering places, news stands below ground next to major train stops, upscale restaurants with bars that I sold P. F. crackers and Goldfish crackers in bulk packages. Some accounts even surprised me as a salesman and a New Yorker. Accounts such as several florists who made gourmet gift baskets and shipped them nation wide and a food service vendor who exclusively sold to cruise ships on the West Side of Manhattan, I sold them all, at lest one of my many items.

Introduction of new items always helps you increase the sales.

This is one of the most common ways that companies increase the sales volume. It's also another advantage of owning a brand name route, as large companies always create new products to boost their sales, as research shows majority of consumers like to try new products. Not every new product becomes a great seller. However it's important to remember that the parent company invested millions of dollars in research, development, packaging, test marketing, and advertising new products, so they rely on you the route owner, to place the new items in every single account that you service. You have to give every new item an opportunity to sell in today's very competitive market.

MY FELLOW READERS ITS ALL UP TO YOU TO MAKE IT HAPPEN.

How bad do you want to succeed?

What time, effort, and necessary sacrifices are you willing to make for the success you want?

Know the area of your route inside and out.

Knock on all the doors that you possibly can, you just don't know of the potential and of all the possibilities that are out there until you do.

Inspirations exist, but it has to find us working.

Pablo Picasso

To further help you increase the sales; expand your selling space in small stores. Since my route was in Manhattan all the stores were small so I had a very limited shelve space.

My goal was where ever possible to place a small metal display rack that company provided free of charge, so this way I could exclusively put only my product on the rack. Just about every account where I placed the rack sales immediately increased. Market place is very competitive, especially in big cities were stores are small, so its important to have an agreement with the owner, as the exact location of the placement of the display rack in the store. It must be close to the front of the store or the main aisles were costumers are walking in the store. Display rack and the product must be visible and easily accessible. In many convenience stores were this was not possible, I kept the small space on the front shelve near the register rather then placing a display rack in back of the store or in the corner. Many of the small stores were open twenty-four hours and seven days a week and product sold very quickly, that I had to service them twice a week, or leave some extra product for them to pack out.

Should you give the first order free of charge to a new small store for a privilege of placing a display rack in front of the store?

You are an independent businessman; it's your decision. You can ask your area manager for his or her opinion and then decide if it's worth it or not. I know that Pepperidge Farm never gave free product to a store. In my many years of experience many storeowners told me, that Frito Lay, which is owned by Pepsi Cola, gave first order free to new stores. That meant is they would place Frito Lay display rack in favorable location in the store and rack would be filled with product free of charge. Frito Lay routes are all company owned routes the drivers work for Frito Lay so they follow instructions. This presented problem for independently owned routes that sold other brands of potatoes chips and pretzels etc. In most cases route owners followed Frito Lay and gave the first order free of charge but had to pay for the product themselves.

Over the years many new storeowners asked me for a first order free but I simply explained to them that Pepperidge Farm does not give free merchandise. I explained to them the quality of our products, the high consumer demand for them, and guaranteed sales. In case the product does not sell by the freshness date stamped on each package he gets full credit for it.

I will provide him with an excellent service and any display rack that he may need free of charge. The delivery is free, with no minimum order that he has to purchase. Its also important to remind him that several of his closest competitors carry the products and is selling very well, and that his customers will be looking for him to also sell it as well. If still not successful, and I wish to reassure him that company policy is no free merchandise. I would hand him the business card of my area manager who he can call to verify if he wishes to do so.

Selling product on consignment to increase the sales?

Selling product on consignment to small stores or any other accounts I would advise you not to do it. You have to pay for the product so why give it to the store to pay you when he sells it. Its better to give the accounts a very small order, of your best selling items, if he never sold your products and is reluctant to try it and get paid C.O.D. Give him your business card and assure him if the product does not sell you will give him a full credit so he has nothing to loose, but gain additional sales.

ANOTHER GOOD IDEA TO INCREASE THE SALES IS TO: "PLAN YOUR WORK AND WORK YOUR PLAN."

Most people in all walks of life don't plan to fail rather they fail to plan. Planning requires time and dedication, but it will pay off for you in time saved and the sales you will gain.

Planning:

- Helps you set specific sales objectives and organize your work to be more productive and efficient.

- Allow you to be proactive rather than reactive.

- Decreases your chances of being caught off guard without enough products.

- Encourages you to execute the best of your abilities because you can set concrete, challenging and attainable goals.

- Write down your specific goals.

- List and analyze the obstacles, which stand in the way of your achieving your goals.

- Think of specific actions you can take to overcome each obstacle and achieve the goal.

- Look for resources of people who could help you overcome each obstacle and achieve the goal.

- Pick realistic targets and completion dates.

- Begin working to meet you goals.

Chapter 20

Don't forget to work with your area manager to help you grow the business that is their job. They are there to assist you in any way they can, to provide sales advice on market trends and conditions as well as upcoming promotions. They are trained sales managers, professionals who daily face problems, situations, obstacles and different circumstances. Then they find answers, solutions and help to resolve the issues.

They are very dedicated hard working individuals who do not get enough recognition or appreciation from the route owners or the parent companies.

There are so many ways to increase the sales on you route that is impossible to write them all, but if you learn to execute the ones I have listed on the daily basis your success will be more, much more the you ever imagined it will be. Maybe one day I will receive a thank you card from you, for helping you on,

"YOUR ROUTE TO SUCCESS"

Building route equity.

- The more you sell the more income you generate for yourself.

- You are selling brand name product that is already a proven seller in the market place.

- As a route owner you have a vested interest in helping to protect and grow your personal investment.

- The best way to achieve both objectives is through a procedure known as Building Route Equity.

- Very simply is to grow your business.

- Right now it is providing income for you and your family.

Sometime in the future as you grow your business, by increasing your service to major accounts and open up new accounts, place many promotional displays, route might also provide you with additional financial rewards, when you sell the route.

The first step needed to build your route equity is by delivering effective reliable service.

Once you build your route equity to the fullest it's up to you to keep it and enjoy the benefits or start looking for other possible routes to purchase were there is a noticeable room for growth and expansion. Then you can sell your route for maximum profit. Like I said many times. Route Business is a beautiful business for a person with a positive attitude, discipline, desire and a good work ethic.

Success over a period of time is waiting for you.

Building Route Equity

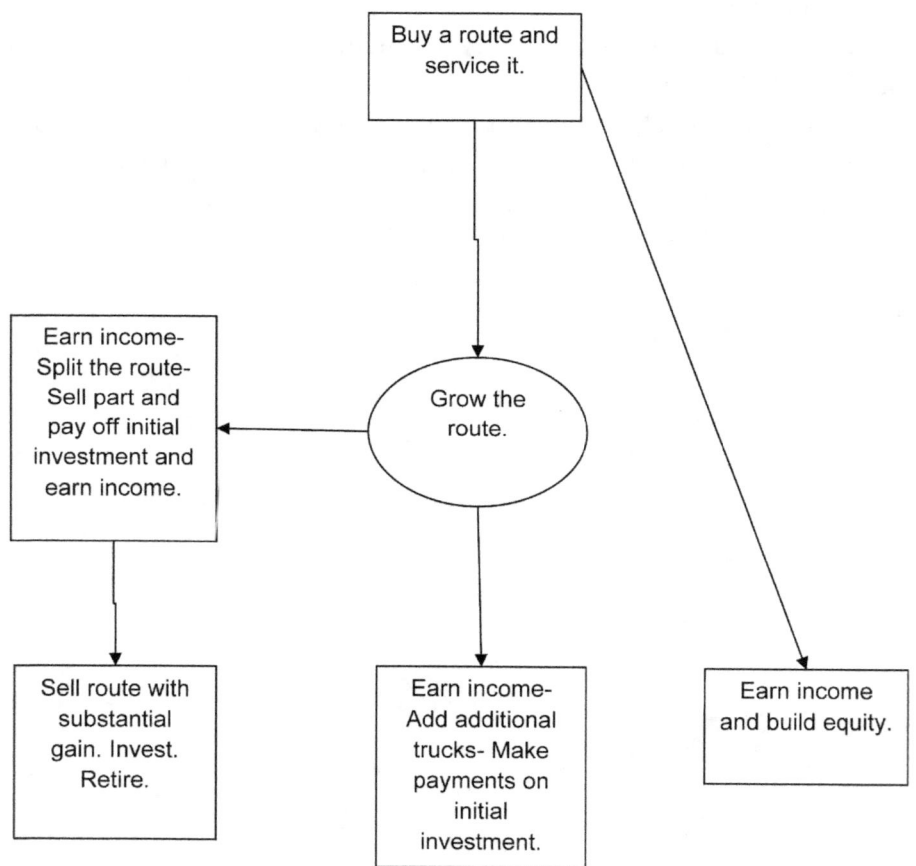

Chapter 21

THANK GOD I SURVIVED THE TWO TERRORISTS ATTACKS WHILE SERVICING THE STORES IN THE WORLD TRADE CENTER COMPLEX.

My route was located in down town Manhattan (N.Y.C.) with World Trade Center located in the middle of it. The business generated directly inside the W .T. C. accounted for about one third of my route's business. In the W.T.C. complex I was servicing F.W. Woolworth, the two Duane Reade Drugstores as well as several news stands located way down underground were the Path Train stop was. Me being a New Yorker most of my life the most surprising sight to me was the amount of people coming through the W.T.C. Complex during the rush our that it seemed to last for hours. It was all orderly and disciplined it almost looked like it was scripted for a movie shoot. I also remember my first delivery to the W.T.C., for a Duane Reade Drugstore a very small store, with an excellent location. Right next to entrance to the W.T.C. and the escalators coming up from the train stop. I had a two-foot section on the end cap with six shelves. At that time they always discounted the Pepperidge Farm Cookies and Crackers. As I rolled in my hand truck full of cookies in to the store and waited for the manager to check the order, he walked up to me and said; "What are you waiting for, that's not enough product. That will be sold out very quickly." That was easy problem to solve. I went quickly, back to my truck and bought in more products.

I learned fast to service the stores in the W.T.C. often and soon as they opened to receive the orders, which was around five in the morning. I would stock the shelves fully and always leave extra product in the back room to be packed out as needed. I was servicing the stores in W.T.C. just about every day because of very limited shelve space, since the stores were small and very busy with so many people working and visiting the W.T.C., and the financial district of Wall Street.

One day in summer of 1993 about nine A.M. it all came to halt, as the first terrorist attack took place on the W.T.C. Complex, with a huge explosion in the underground parking garage. Several people died and many were injured. Thankfully I was servicing the stores very early in the morning so I left the complex before the explosion. I was in the area servicing other stores and I did witness thousands of people running out of the buildings and very dark clouds of smoke coming out of the exits and entrances to the buildings underground garages. Within minutes emergency personnel from many different agencies were coming from all directions to help. For a moment I simply froze in my truck, like every body else in their cars around me. We all quickly realized we had to move to the side to let the emergency vehicles through, and then leave the area so all the emergency personnel can do their job. Thank God the explosion did not cause a major damage to the W.T.C. Complex. The following day was a clean up day and further security measures and more restrictions to underground garage parking including the commercial delivery vehicles were put in place. From then on to be able to park my step van in to the W.T.C. commercial vehicles area only. I had to wait in line, and walk to their security booth with my drivers license, get the picture taken and show them the stores invoice that I am delivering to. To bring back the business to normal it took several weeks and very effective sales promotions by all the W.T.C. merchants participating.

New Yorkers are resilient and hard working people that are not easily scared from going about their business and proceed to normal life. I serviced the W.T.C. for another eight years, thank God with out any problems. Then late in 1999 a fellow route owner with whom I developed friendship decided that he would sell his route in midtown Manhattan and retire. He asked me would I be interested in buying his route. He knew of my complaints about the traffic, congestion, and difficulties in parking my truck to service the accounts on my route. He was well aware of this when on occasion he serviced my route for a day or two while I was on a vacation. One day we planed that I go with him on his route to see the area and the accounts he serviced. After only a few hours on the route with him I noticed that his area is less congested with traffic and it's much easier to park the truck and service the stores. His average weekly sales were close to mine, so it wasn't like I was going to be making less money. Simple handshake sealed the deal for me to buy his route as soon as I sell my route. It took several months for me to sell my route to a former Wise Potato Chips route owner. He liked the Pepperidge Farm products and the idea of protected territory type of route, rather then protected accounts type of route. Protected accounts type of route, stores are scattered all over the city so you spend a lot of time in driving from one to another.

Approximately two years later 9/11/2001 we all know what happened, especially New Yorkers. We, the citizens of this great country of hours and all the people of good will around the world should never forget what took place.

I know I will not forget for as long as I live.

To those who lost there loved ones, my personal condolences to you. May God give you strength each and every day to live your life, as your loved one would want you to?

I am happy to say the fellow who bought my route did not get hurt that day, as he serviced the stores in the W.T.C. very early in the morning like I used to do. Terrorist attack took place later around nine in the morning. He told me he was only two blocks away when the first plane struck one of the towers, and when a large piece of metal fell by his truck, that he got so scared he wisely immediately started driving away, towards a Williamsburg Bridge to leave Manhattan.

I think every single American remembers where he or she was that morning of 9/11/2001. The exact place where they were and what they were doing. If I may speak for all New Yorkers we for sure, with out any doubt in our mind know the exact place where we were and what we were doing at that moment the W.T.C. came under terrorist attack. Me being an eyewitness of an attack and for months later seeing the rescue operation taking place and the clean up, and all the extra security measures I had to go through, because my route was in the city. You can bet your life I know where I was and what I was doing at time of the terrorist attack. I will never forget it as long as I live. I was servicing the supermarket (Food Emporium) on Third Avenue and thirty second street near the Midtown Tunnel. Within half an hour of the attack as I was packing out my order, the store got so full of people like I never saw before. People were buying everything, especially bread, milk, eggs, ice cubes and so on. It felt like we were being invaded, like World War Three was on our doorstep. As I quickly finished packing out my order I wanted to get to my truck and listen to the radio, as customers were telling me contradicting stories on what had occurred. Some were telling me one plane and that it was an accident, others said it was a large gas explosion, I didn't know what to believe, until I heard people saying that a second plane hit the W.T.C. Towers. As I almost had to fight my way through the store full of people the store manager noticed me. He, and almost all of his employees were at the check out lines packing the groceries to get the customers out as quickly as possible, as more and more people were coming in to the store. He yelled to me; "come on Barry give us a hand for ten minutes you cant go anywhere, all the bridges and tunnels are closed and traffic is at a stand still in all of Manhattan." That ten minutes help turned into half hour. I noticed most of the people were anxious, nervous, upset, frightened, with a worried, and scared look on their face all in a big hurry to get home and get the information on what is happening, who is doing this, and why are they doing it. I told the store manager "I am only few blocks from the Midtown Tunnel I will take my chances in trying to get to it. They have to open it soon or later." I found out later that they closed all the tunnels in the area, as a precaution, just in case there are terrorist driving a truck loaded with explosives.

   As I got out of the store I looked towards downtown, the direction of the Twin Towers and as far as I could see I saw both sides of Third Avenue jammed with people walking so fast as if they were running for their lives. All of them with sweat, worried, anxious, frightened look on their faces, watery eyes and many with visible tears coming down their face. Men with loose ties, jackets over their shoulder, shirt hanging out, many with sneakers on as they found out that trains will not be running, from fear of explosives being on the trains. Ladies with a noticeable mascara on their face as tears kept coming down their face, with hair ruffled and clothes looking like they were just attacked. They all marched forward quickly as if they were on some kind of mission. Some of them were walking barefooted, especially the ladies who lost their heels and shoes in walking for such a long distance from a financial district. Buses and taxis could not go any were as the traffic was at a standstill. I just froze in disbelief of what I was witnessing in front of me, with a hand truck in my one hand and a hand held computer in the other and with thousands of people marching towards me I was concerned not to be hit like a ball in a pinball machine.

It was a sunny clear day not a cloud in the sky, except the dark smoke that covered large area of the sky over the Twin Towers and forming huge clouds that were grey, very dark, and some so black as if the nastiest off storms was going to start. It was visible for miles and miles all over the tri state area. I could not believe what was happening, and there was nothing I could do. I felt helpless. Somehow I managed to get to my step van, which was half a block away. I quickly put on the radio. Store manager was right I could not go any were, traffic was at standstill as far as I could see in all directions. For about half an hour I was glued to the radio changing from one station to another to hear the latest news or at least a confirmation at what the other station was saying really did happen. It finally occurred to me to contact my family to let them know that I am all right.

Millions of people had the same idea in mind and phone service was dead. Since I was only few blocks from the Midtown Tunnel I finally attempted to get to it. It took me about one hour to move two blocks. Then I was told by the traffic agent to go to a line with all other commercial vehicles. There was no movement of a long line off commercial vehicles so I shut off the engine and stepped out of my step van. As I got out a fellow diver standing by his tuck told me that police have orders not to allow any commercial vehicles through the tunnel. I locked my step van and walked about two hundred yards to the very entrance to the tunnel. There I noticed thousands of people waiting in lines as police officers stopped all the cars to take as many people as they can fit, through the tunnel and drop them off in Queens, were the buses and trains were operating. I was able to speak to one of the police officers and explain to him that I have a step van and that I could probably fit fifteen to twenty people in. He answered, "My orders are not to let any commercial vehicles through." I went back to my vehicle and sat there for one to two hours in hoping that they will let us go through. I was listening to the news and finally heard that commercial vehicles must use the bridges to exit Manhattan. The fear was of a truck loaded with explosives, exploding in the tunnels under the water on the east and the west side of Manhattan would cause unimaginable number of deaths and destruction. The Fifty Ninth Street Bridge was closest to me. It took me three to four hours to get to it, as it seemed as I was crawling my way there rather then driving. Thank God I arrived home safely about six o clock in the evening. It's a day that will stay fresh in my mind as long as I live.

For years after the attack all the route owners servicing stores in Manhattan, as well as drivers of all commercial vehicles coming to the city were reminded of that day by randomly being pulled over by the police officers and have their trucks inspected for possible explosives. The fellow that bought my route lost a lot of business due to the terrorist attack. He did tell me that Pepperidge Farm did provide him with some help. He continued to work hard and stay positive and optimistic. Short time later he bought a small route next to his area to help him in recovery of the loss in the business. I am happy to tell you that as of this writing September 2012, that he is still working, and looking forward to a new W.T.C. being build. Right now the One World Trade Center Tower is almost completed.

The reason for me writing this chapter about the W.T.C. terrorist attack is, as I was going through my route business paper work, I came across The Temporary Parking Permit for a delivery to W.T.C. stores. It automatically brought all the memories of that horrible day back to me. The events and the people I did business with for so many years, it all started to flash in my mind, and in front of my eyes like it was yesterday. My fellow readers you just cannot forget, it doesn't matter how hard you try to forget it. So I had to write it, and tell you about my experience, and for one more time to thank God for keeping me safe not on one but both terrorist attacks.

With my story and this simple; Temporary Parking Permit to W.T.C. that I pay my tribute to thousands who lost their lives on that day and to all their loved ones left behind;

"May God bless you and give you strength to go on with your lives as you lost so much and suffered so long."

To thousands brave men and woman who took part in rescue and later in the clean up of the W.T.C. site, so that the lives of millions of New Yorker's would get back to normal as soon as possible.

I say; "THANK YOU, THANK YOU, MAY GOD BLESS YOU ALL AND MAY GOD BLESS AMERICA "still the greatest, richest, most powerful, most generous country in the world."

Chapter 21

WORLD TRADE CENTER
TRUCK DOCK
TEMPORARY PARKING PERMIT

1) COMMERCIAL VEHICLES ONLY

2) PARK IN MARKED SPACES ONLY

3) THIRTY MINUTE TIME LIMIT

4) TIME BEGINS AT VALIDATION

5) PERMIT MUST BE TOTALLY VISIBLE IN WINDSHIELD

6) VIOLATORS WILL BE IMMOBILIZED BY AUTO CLAMP

TIME IN: 05 33 06 NOV 98

WTC RAMP E
20 NOV 98

Chapter 22

YOUR ROUTE TO SUCCESS DEPENDS ON YOU STAYING HEALTHY, OPTIMISTIC, POSITIVE, IN A VERY COMPETITIVE, MARKET PLACE.

I don't have to tell you we live in a very competitive world and often a very negative, uncivil one. With escalating vulgarity, lax standards, sensational media were anything goes, in magazines and newspapers for more sales and television for higher ratings in viewership. To keep my self in a positive frame of mind it was and is a challenge every day. Having a route in N.Y.C. and living in the media capital of the world made it that much challenging, to stay focused, optimistic, positive and enthusiastic day in and day out.

What I did is I placed many positive and motivating articles, and inspiring messages for myself in the truck so they will constantly be practically in my face to able to read over and over. This chapter is all about the importance of being and staying positive, optimistic, and thinking healthy thoughts. I am certain that there is no way that I would have accomplished the goals I set out for myself while owning a route business with out taking care of myself, my body, my mind and my soul. To have good health these need to work with not against each other. I thanked God every single day for providing me with good health so I can take care of my business. I believe that in over twenty one years of route business ownership I might have lost total of ten to fifteen days do to not feeling well.

Every single day and through out the day I would repeat out loud to my self; "I feel great, I am a happy and healthy person and I live a meaningful life. "Happy and healthy person feels terrific."

We all become like that with which we live like, that which we look upon, read or hear. If we like beautiful things we become beautiful in our spirit. The type of attitude you have and you present every day in dealing with storeowners and managers, in time will definitely have a positive or negative impact on your earnings. Just about all of my accounts were happy to see me, they greeted me well; with a smile, friendly hand shake, pat on the back or an enthusiastic hello. Over time not only did I created a positive friendly atmosphere in my accounts, that helped me stay motivated and positive but it helped me increase the sales by gaining more selling space in smaller stores. In the chain stores it helped me increase the sales with placements of promotional displays in higher traffic areas in the store.

***Be optimistic, enthusiastic and think healthy thoughts.** Our health largely depends on what we harbor in our minds. Keep free of any kind of guilt. Remember my saying through out the book: "To do the right thing." Wrongdoing can actually plant the seed of sickness in the soul. Then that illness proceeds to adversely affect the mind and, in time the body. In case you have a feeling of guilt, you should get rid of it in order to feel healthy. Along with staying free of guilt try to empty your mind of all hate thoughts, defeat thoughts, mean or negative thoughts. To have good health, think healthy thoughts and positive emotions. Emotion of; desire, faith love, enthusiasm, romance and of hope. Another step to good health is to affirm the life force. God's life force is in you, the more you affirm this the more powerfully it will flow in you. Repeat often; "I see myself as whole, with my body functioning perfect in harmony with God's perfect laws. My whole being is fulfilled with health. In him is life; His life is in me.[3]*

---

3 Three Ways To Good Health by Dr. Norman Vincent Peale

Every day in every way by the grace of God I am getting better and better."

Dr. Emile Coves

MAKE A HABIT OF PRACTICING KINDNESS, GENEROSITY, AND GRATITUDE, BEING HELPFUL ENTHUSIASTIC, RESPONSIBLE AND RELIABLE. PEOPLE WHO REGULARLY ENGAGE IN THESE ACTS AND MAKE A HABIT OF IT LIVE LONGER, HEALTHIER, HAPPIER AND MORE SUCCESSFUL LIVES.

We seldom think of what we have. Rather of what we lack. It's a great tragedy.

Dale Carnegie

This just reminded me of another saying I had written in the truck; I had the blues because I had no shoes. Until upon the street, I met a man who had no feet.
   Count your blessings.
   Health is wealth.

Here are some notes and articles that I had placed in my truck to keep me in the right frame of mind while working on the route in N.Y.C. The city that never sleeps and the city and its people that I will always be grateful to for an opportunity I had to make my and my families life a better one.

I WILL ACT NOW

When the lion is hungry he eats
When the eagle is thirsty he drinks
Unless they act they both will perish
I hunger for success,
I thirst for happiness and peace of mind
Unless I act, I will perish in life of failure

misery and sleepless nights
I will command and obey my own command
Action is the food and drink that will nourish my success
Source unknown

I will not be denied the success that is rightfully mine.
I promise myself to be so strong that nothing will upset my peace of mind.
I promise myself to talk health, happiness and prosperity to everyone I meet.
I promise myself to forget the mistakes of the past and press on to the greater achievements of the future.
I promise my self to give so much time to the improvement of myself that I have no time to criticize others.
Source unknown

All good things come to he who hopes.
For all hopes lead to
Dreams of success
To fulfill dreams of success
Develop a plan of action
Act on the plan and work consistently, all consistent work is called persistence, persistence leads to success.

I   FEEL   GREAT

I am a happy and healthy person and I live a meaningful life.
I wake up in the morning full of energy, vitality,
content and feeling absolutely great.
I go through the day with energy
A bounce in my step, a smile on my face
I don't feel stressed, anxious, depressed or tired
I have no headaches, or pain in my body.
I have strength and tone in my muscles
My body is fluid, graceful, flexible firm, strong and vibrant.
I go to sleep at night and sleep soundly, peacefully,
and get a whole nights rest.
Feeling great. Happy and healthy.

Joyfully content with my life, by the grace of God.
Source unknown

Winners are people like you.

- Winners take chances.

- Like everyone else, they fear failing, but they refuse to let fear control them.

- Winners don't give up.

- When life gets rough, they hang in until the going gets better.

- Winners are flexible.

- They realize there is more than one way and are willing to try others.

- Winners know they are not perfect.

- They respect their weaknesses while making the most of their strengths.

- Winners fall, but hey don't stay down.

- They stubbornly refuse to let a fall keep them from climbing.

- Winners don't blame fate for their failures or luck for their success.

- Winners accept responsibility for their lives.

- Winners are positive thinkers who see good in all things.

- From the ordinary, they make the extra ordinary.

- Winners believe in the path they have chosen.

- Even when it's hard, even when others can't see where they are going, winners are patient.

- They know a goal is only as worthy as the effort that's required to achieve it.

- Winners are people like you.

- They make this world a better place to be.

Source unknown

Chapter 23

DON'T BUY A ROUTE IF........

Maybe that's too strong of a statement or harsh. Better question would be to think twice about buying a route, or simply think it over if:

1. You find it difficult to deal or get along with all kinds of people. Route Business is a peoples business.
   Your attitude is everything.

2. If you cannot get up early every morning and develop a schedule, a routine and follow it day in and day out. It comes down to planning your work and working your plan. Yes I know it sounds very simple, easy, basic, common sense, a routine, but its sad, pathetic, unprofessional and unproductive in how many times I saw a route owner, while working as a district manager and as a route business owner after several deliveries siting in the drivers seat, thinking where to go next, and which stop to do.

3. If you are not a self-starter, a go-getter.
   You are investing your hard earned money into a business. If that does not motivate you to become a self-starter, a go-getter, then I don't know what will. If you are not, then look for a job were the boss will tell you what time to be at work, what to do, the time to take lunch, when is the break time, and the time to go home.

4. If your desire and plan to grow the business is not there from the very first day it wont be there next year or five years from now.

5. Be honest and realistic to yourself. If you think that you cannot and won't be able to do what the present route owner is doing while he is showing you the route for a week or two, then don't buy the route.
   You may end up loosing part of your investment.

Life isn't about finding yourself. Life is about creating yourself.

George Bernard Shaw

Chapter 24

MY SECRETS TO SUCCESS?

The truth and the reality fellow readers is that if being successful was easy everybody would be successful. Success before work only comes in a dictionary.

Elevator to success is out of order. You have to use the stairs one step at the time.

If you like the route business, were the more you selling the more money you will make. You have to be prepared to wear many hats; that of a salesman, businessman, driver, delivery man, merchandiser and more. My hope and wish is that with My Secrets To Success to further help you to succeed in owning a route business or any other small business. My advice to you is to read this chapter often to stay motivated, inspired, with a can do attitude to keep striving towards your goals and success that you want.

You are a salesman. One of your many goals should be to make people on the route like you, easy to get along with and happy to see you. People like storeowners, managers, assistant managers, store receivers, your district manager, basically everybody you work with while operating your business. Very simply at the end of the day, it pays to be liked, easy to get along with, a person happy to see, a person that's good, that always tries to do good and expects the good.

My Secrets To Success?

How to make people like you?

1. Become interested in people. (Talk about them.)

2. Smile.

3. Remember names.

4. Be a good listener.

5. Make everyone feel important.

6. Give sincere compliments.

You can make more friends in two months by becoming really interested in other people, than you can in two years by trying to get other people interested in you.

Dale Carnegie

Build your reputation.

1. Be honest and truthful.

2. Be a leader.

3. Be helpful, show, teach, set an example.

4. Look, act and feel successful.

5. Walk faster; smile bigger, act friendlier, dress well.

6. Be enthusiastic

Act and be self-confident.

> 1. I am successful.
>
> 2. I have a meaningful life.
>
> 3. I can overcome fear and worry.
>
> 4. I can pull the curtain on the past and burn my weak bridges.
>
> 5. I am self-disciplined. Knowing I have a job or a task to complete. Then having the drive and desire to complete it.

My pattern of success.

> 1. I will not wait until all the conditions are right for me to become successful. I might wait rest of my life.
>
> 2. There is no right age or perfect time to be successful.
>
> 3. I am ready to start right now. I have the desire, motivation, and attitude to work and courage to take the next step.
>
> 4. I will not depend on someone else for success for they might depend on me.
>
> 5. I will use efficiency the qualities and knowledge I have.
>
> 6. I will not fear failure to fail only shows I have been trying.
>
> 7. It matters not how many times I fail but how quickly I get up.

My Secrets To Success?

Six most important areas of my life
    Home and family - physically
    Financially - socially
    Spiritually - mentally

  Where do I stand now in all my areas of life?
  Evaluate my strengths and weaknesses.

  What are my goals?

  Do I know my short and long term goals?
  Determine what specific goals you want to achieve?
  To be able to achieve any of the goals you set out for yourself to achieve. You must be able to answer; WHAT do you want? WHEN do you want it?
  WHERE are you going to get the (what you want)?
  HOW are you going to get it?
  Your goals must be written down clearly.
  Example; I would like to buy a route business in the next six months, or I want to increase my weekly sales by ten percent.
  I now have the answer to" WHAT "do I want?
  I want to buy the route business.
  I also decided on" WHEN "do I want to buy the route business?
  Within the next six months. I set out a deadline for my self in reaching my goal of buying the route business. It is so important to write it down and place the notice in a location that you will see it often.
  To reach the goal, on increasing the weekly sales by ten percent.
  My decision is to start immediately on a plan, of HOW and "WHERE" to make this happen. I will write down the name of the accounts WHERE I feel that I have a definite possibility on increasing their weekly sales.
  "HOW "exactly am I going to increase the sales?
  I have to be specific, in all the actions I plan to take, to reach my goal in increasing the weekly sales and make more money.
  I will increase the number of times a week I service my key accounts.

I will try to place permanent secondary displays in three of my best stores.

On my weekly promotions I will try my very best to place more promotional displays.

When I fully complete my day's work, I will stop by the potential new account that I saw the other day.

If you answered ALL the questions honestly and realistically, you have greatly increased the chance of not only reaching your goal but in most cases surpassing it and achieving it quicker.

THE WHAT, WHEN, WHERE, AND HOW ARE YOUR STEPPING STONES TO; "YOUR ROUTE TO SUCCESS "IN OWNING ANY SMALL BUSINESS.

We tend to draw to ourselves that which we sat out from ourselves.

We become precisely what we imagine ourselves to be.

When your goals are clear and vivid they act as magnet and they draw you to them.

If you know there is a build in situation or any obstacle, plan to go through it, around it, or to eliminate the situation or any obstacle.

Think and Grow Rich By Author Napoleon Hill

Through out every day repeat to yourself a powerful motivational statement:

"I WILL NOT BE DENIED THE SUCCESS THAT'S RIGHTFULLY MINE."

Develop sincere desire for the things you want in life.

Burning desire is the greatest motivator of human actions.

To further help you on your road to success in reaching your goals.

Ask yourself following questions;

My Secrets To Success?

1. What are the obstacles and roadblocks that I will personally have to overcome to achieve my goals?
Am I willing to make the necessary sacrifices?
Think about them very carefully and write them down.
Be honest and realistic.
2. What are the rewards for me personally, when I attain them?
3. Is it worth it to me?
Answer them completely, honestly and realistically.

This will help you develop a supreme confidence in yourself and your ability. Confidence comes from experience.
Experience comes from, know how.
Know how comes from having the courage to submit yourself to obstacles, situations and circumstances that an average person shy's away from.

Every time you say, "I can do it and I will do it."
You are strengthening your determination and resolve.

> It doesn't matter how much you know. But what does is what you do with it.
> All things are possible for those who believe it.
> You must have absolute belief.
> Persistence will always overcome resistance.
> It is my attitude that determines everything I experiment in life.
> Law of attraction is that what we attract, what we think.
> You become what you think about the most.
> Positive thoughts are the basis for a success attitude.
> Success habits, that lead, directly to positive expectancy's in everything, I do.

Your self-image.
Self-image is the key to human personality and human behavior.
Change the self-image and you change the personality and the behavior.
The self-image sets boundaries of individual accomplishment.
It defines what you can do and cannot do.

Positive attitude with positive thinking does indeed work when its consistent with individual self image.

From book, Psycho Cybernetics by Dr. Maxwell Malts

    Success in selling requires ambition, ability, drive, and superior knowledge of your products, services, and company selling methods.
    It also requires the ability to endure a failure in opening up a new account or getting an approval from the store manager for a front-end display of you products. The key is to stay focused and be optimistic.
    Look at the long-term plan of your business.
    Make it your goal to enjoy your work.
    If you do, you will sell more, and find it easier to reach your goals and success you have planed for yourself.

Success is a matter of understanding and religiously practicing specific, simple habits that always lead to success.

                            Robert J. Ringer
                      Author of Million Dollar Habits

LADDER OF SUCCESS*

100% I DID.

90% I WILL.

80% I CAN.

70% I THINK I MIGHT.

60% I MIGHT.

50% I THINK I CAN.

40% I COULD.

30% I WISH I COULD.

20% I DON'T KNOW HOW.

10% I CAN'T.

*(Source unknown)

WHERE DO YOU STAND?
Be honest, realistic, and plan to improve.

Success can be reduced to a formula:

Determine the principles, which bring success and those, which bring failure.

Employ the principles that bring success and avoid those which bring failure.

Example;

You just bought a route that is averaging eight thousand dollars in weekly sales. Your immediate plan is to copy all the principles from the seller that he is using to keep those sales coming every week.

Once you did that successfully, then you improve, and build on his success principles.

Another principle to Your Route To Success is; Self Discipline.

The single most important characteristic you need to succeed at anything you try is

Self discipline.

It's the development of self –control, character, being organized efficient.

Following simple tips can help you develop self-discipline.

*Find a role model.

Copy success.

All the great people through out history had enormous self-discipline.

So pick a famous person, try one in the same field you're in and learn all you can about him.

As you study how he achieved his goals, and imitate his self-discipline, that self-discipline will become part of you.

My Secrets To Success?

*Don't look back.

Often people assume past failures, mistakes, setbacks will prevent future success, but the past won't affect the future unless you let it.

*Learn to enjoy challenges.

View problems, situations, and obstacles as challenges you can overcome.

To help you along write down and review all you're past successes.

View them just as another stepping-stone or a roadblock on your road to success.

Learn from yesterday, live for today, hope for tomorrow.

Albert Einstein

*Develop concentration.

When distracting thoughts come to mind and you are facing so many challenges at once simply stop.

Find a quiet place, close your eyes, relax and take several deep breaths, exhale very slowly and focus only on one thought, your own well-being, and only on ONE most important job that needs to be done now.

Learn to prioritize.

*Always look at your long-term business plan. Watch the calendar not the clock.

The self-disciplined person doesn't measure time with a stopwatch but with a calendar.

Planning a series of goals that may take weeks or months as a way of reaching an ultimate goal.

*Be an optimist.

Develop and use positive thinking.

Put failure out of your mind and replace it with thoughts of success.

How to succeed?
What to do next to help you succeed?
You'll move in the direction of your thoughts.
You become what you think about most.

We must become the change we want to see.

Mahatma Gandhi

*Sit back, relax, and use creative daydreaming.

What is it you want yourself discipline to help you accomplish?
Visualize a picture in your mind of exactly what things will be like when you achieve your goal.
Write it all down it has to be realistic and attainable.

*Don't try to be perfect.

Plan ways to succeed in small goals that you can accomplish.
Then use this success to build confidence in yourself, your abilities, a can do attitude to even greater success in near future.

*Balance your life.

Self discipline means you know when to play as well as when to work towards your goals. If you try to be self-disciplined every second of every day, you'll be like a man sitting on a two –legged stool, bound to fall off.
Life is divided into three major components, work, play, and love.
Don't ignore any one of them or you'll be sitting on a two-legged stool.

Should you make a decision to buy the route business or not.
My secrets to success will help you in any business you choose, as well as make a positive difference in your life.

My Secrets To Success?

1. Determine what specific goal you want to achieve.
Write down your plan to reach it.
Then totally dedicate yourself to its achievement.
2. How you think is everything on the road to success.
Strive to be positive, optimistic, learn to look at the bright side of everything.
Beware, and avoid negative people.
3. Develop a plan for achieving your goal and take action.
Goals are nothing with out action.
Write down your plan and progress.
Create a to do list, hour-by-hour, day-by-day, month-by-month.
4. Your goal must be what you think about most.
Then you will develop a sincere desire for the goal you planned to achieve.

> Sincere, burning desire motivates you to take action and further help you in building other habits of success.

5. Success is a journey not a destination.
Be prepared to work hard, persistent and resilient.
6. Develop discipline and a supreme confidence in yourself and your abilities.

> Concentrate on your passed successes and strengths, instead on passed failures or setbacks and weaknesses.

Think and concentrate on solutions instead of your problems.
7. Get training and never stop learning.
Read books or go back to school if necessary.
8. Stay focused on your goal your plan and time and money.

> Be strong disciplined and focused, don't let other people or things distract you from what is important to you.

9. View any failures as temporary setbacks.
Learn from your setbacks, and your mistakes.
They all carry with them lesson to be learned.

A lesson of an equal, or greater benefit, in near future's successes.

> Be determined to follow through on your plan, regardless of obstacles, circumstances, or criticism from others. Many people quit or simply give up too soon on their plan, with out realizing the success, just may be around the corner.

10. Take responsibility for your actions and inactions, setbacks and successes.

> Your success, happiness, health, well-being, and financial security; It's all up to you. Nobody else but you.

> Take responsibility, be honest, realist, and dependable. Otherwise No's 1-9 won't matter to you and your; goal, plan, success, family, relatives, friends, your own future and well-being.

SUCCESS CAN BE BOILED DOWN TO THREE SIMPLE THINGS; DECISIONS, PRIORITIES AND ACTION.

People who routinely make bad decisions, have misplaced priorities, and fail to take action are generally prone to failure. However, people who exercise sound judgment, set priorities based on importance, and take action are usually successful.

The point that I am making here is that success isn't going to just miraculously come to you as a result of wishful thinking. Instead, you must choose to be successful, and if you're really serious about being a successful owner of a route business (or any business) you must make a conscientious decision to do so, set your priorities accordingly, and then follow everything up with action.

There are three types of people in the world; people that make things happen, people that watch things happen, and people that don't know what is happening.

My Secrets To Success?

It's up to you to decide what group of people you wish to be with.

Weakness of attitude becomes weakness of character.
Albert Einstein

Successful people believe.

I create my life.
Unsuccessful people believe.
Life happens to them.
You have to believe that you are the one who creates your success, your mediocrity, and your setbacks.
Consciously or unconsciously it's you.
You have to take the responsibility for your thoughts, actions and the end result.

Unsuccessful people blame everything and everyone for their failures, except themselves.

They think the problem is anything or anyone but them.
It's your choice to choose to think in ways that will support you in your happiness and success, instead of failure and unhappiness.
The fact is that your character, your thinking, and your beliefs are a critical part of what determines the level of your success.
Your income can grow only to the extent you do.

If your actions create a legacy that inspires others to dream more, learn more, do more, and become more, then you are an excellent leader.

John Quincy Adams

Chapter 25

MY DISTRIBUTOR/SDA OF THE YEAR AWARD

Mike Salzberg
Vice President – Sales

February 4, 2002

Mr. Barry Strk

Mr. Strk:

Congratulations on winning the top award for Biscuit SDAs for Fiscal 2001 -- the prestigious **Regional Sales Development Associate of the Year Award**. Your efforts during F'01 were outstanding and contributed to the success of the Metro Region and the Pepperidge Farm Sales Organization, nationally. It is single-minded focus such as yours toward superior service, execution, persistence, high visibility on the streets, and strong relationships with customers that lead a DSD organization to success.

It is with great pleasure that I present you the enclosed Savings Bond as a reward for your extraordinary efforts and success.

I look forward to working with you in the marketplace and seeing continued excellent results from your area.

Again, congratulations, and thank you for your strong performance.

Good selling!

Enclosure

Cc: D. L. Albright
F. Jefferson

PEPPERIDGE FARM, INC. 595 Westport Avenue · Norwalk, CT 06851-4482 · 203 846.7000 · Fax 203 846.7369

Chapter 26

PERSONAL FINANCIAL GROWTH CHART.

Level 1. Survive and strive independently.

Level 2. Build security with a nest egg.

Level 3. Grow wealth through investments.

Level 4. Reap the benefits of your hard work.

Object of your winning game plan is to get to Level 4 just as fast as possible.
   To enjoy the benefits of your hard work, accomplishments, and your creations, and be able to face the world boldly, and say;

"This with Gods help I have done."

"Money is only a tool to help you enjoy life."

"Your life is not a tool to just make money."

Chapter 27

FINANCIAL INDEPENDENCE AND REACHING A POINT OF HAVING ENOUGH.

I decided to retire because I felt I have reached a point in my life where I have what I need, and to be able to have time to enjoy what I build and have.

I can honestly say; "I am happy and content."

Being financially secured means having saved enough to meet monthly expenses and living on income from all your investments.

It has nothing to do with how rich or wealthy you are, it's simply a joyful, satisfying, and comforting experience of having enough.[4]

Just few of many advantages that your financial independence provides you with:

*Peace of mind.

With your finances in order, fear and anxiety of not having enough fades.

---

4 'Your Money or Your Life' by Vicki Robin and Joe Dominguez

There is time and space to explore and grow, at your own pace with out any stress and pressure.

*Being out of debt.

What a great feeling, a kind of relief, and a commitment not to return to debt.

*Money saved.

With savings, you will feel secure that, should unforeseen illness or emergency arise, your life will not fall apart.

*Hobbies and skills.

With extra time and freedom, you start new hobbies; develop new skills that make joyful contentment in your life.
    Start cooking natural healthy meals, maybe grow your own vegetables or volunteer in your community.
    Maybe write a book or a guide like me, about your own expertise, experiences and what ever you are passionate about.

Chapter 28
YOUR THINKING AND BELIEFS BEFORE READING THE BOOK?

1. You like most of the people worried about job and income security?

2. You never thought of, or dreamed that you could ever be your own boss?

3. You didn't think that you could own a small business without employees?

4. You thought you needed a lot of money, and to have the experience in owning a small business?

5. You were not sure what you wanted to do?

6. You blamed everyone and everything for your lack of success?

7. You thought that you could never reach financial independence?

8. You were led to believe that you needed a college degree to own a business and to make more money?

9. You lived paycheck to paycheck never saved any money?

10. You let the big, (bad for you), negative media influence your thinking, to accept the tough economic times, as bleak opportunity for a good job, or to start a small business?

As every day far to many of us, think, hope, and rely on, the belief that a government is going to provide for us, and solve all of our problems?

All that we are is the result of what we thought.

Buddha

Chapter 29
YOUR THINKING AND BELIEFS AFTER READING THIS BOOK?

Now you can make the necessary changes and be the better more successful you.

My sincere hope and wish is that I made a positive difference in your way of thinking, in making better choices, in taking positive actions, all in direction to be better more successful person that we both know you can be. From now on, to take personal responsibility, of how you think, choices you make, and the actions you take, that will give you the results, and outcomes you wished, hoped, and dreamed, results and outcomes that you can truly be proud of.

Answers, solutions, results, and possible outcomes, for the way you were led to think and believe.

1. After reading the book thoroughly and understanding its message fully, I would hope and expect you to, if not totally eliminate the worry about the job and income security, at least be far less concern about it. The core message of the book, besides the route business, is that opportunities to better yourself, exists only to the extent that you are willing to accept and believe.

When you start using the habits and principles that lead you to success on daily basis and continue to build on them, step by step, overtime the success and financial rewards will be there for you, just as they were there for me and hundreds of small successful financially independent individuals I met, observed, and learned from.

2. Most people never thought or dreamed that they could ever work for themselves and be their own boss. As you can see from reading the book its not impossible and far from it. In case you disagree, please read the book over very slowly, someplace quiet with out being disturbed. Take a pen and paper and write things down that you find important or answers to your questions, concerns, or any doubts. I am not suggesting that is easy, with out risk, sacrifices and hard work to be self-employed. In long term it pays off for most people, if it wasn't rewarding in so many ways like; job and income security, in being your own boss, freedom and flexibility it provides, and so many other things, then there would be no small businesses all over the world. The fact is, that most successful people make their money, in owning a business. I hope that I changed your mind, and made you believe as well as provided you with self-confidence that you really can own a route business or any other small business.

3. There are many small businesses were you don't need employees; a Route Business is a perfect example of such a business. Naturally all small business owners try their best to grow and expand their business so that they have a need and can afford to hire employees. Any business you start with a limited capital, the key to your success is to keep your expenses and overhead to the very smallest that's possible.

4. Society as a whole always told us, or led us to believe that you need a lot of money and must have experience to start a business. That myth or belief scares too many people, and holds them back from ever thinking let alone looking into a possibility in going into their own business. As you learned from reading the book, the small route business you can buy for as little as fifty thousand dollars down with good credit, and in some instances even less then that. If for whatever the reason you just don't like the route business, don't give up. Continue to work hard and diligently save your money for a small business of your own, and keep actively searching, pursuing

your dream of business ownership. Having any experience in the field or a profession you are looking to start a small business in is a tremendous plus and a great advantage. You must have the confidence in the business as well as in yourself that you have what ever it takes to succeed in the small business you choose. I explained in great detail that route business is special and unique in a way in which it is very simple to learn and operate, while distributing already proven, great brand name products.

5. Many people go through good part of their life not knowing or being able to figure out what they want to do in life.
What is your purpose in life? What do you want to do?
What do you want to achieve? What do you want to have?
What positive changes you wish to make?
Through out the book I wrote about many of my own experiences in jobs and businesses that I tried on my own road to success and financial independence. What I wanted more then anything else in the world, was to be; successful, rich, own my own business, be independent, self reliant, entrepreneur, a go getter, to create my own life, have my own house, my own car, and so on. One of the easiest and surest way to begin clarifying what you truly want is to make a list of things you want to do, things you want to have. Write it all down, you can narrow it down later, consult a spouse, a close relative or a good friend to help you with the list. Review the list often and focus on the things that are real, meaningful, things that you truly believe in, have deep desire, and passion for.

In discovering, deciding, acknowledging and knowing this purpose, this want, and your desire, is the single most important action successful people take. The earlier in life you discover and decide on this, the quicker you will be on your road to success and financial independence. I knew what I wanted. I was clear, beyond any doubt in my mind on what I wanted and what I wish to accomplish. I did not wait, hope, or wish for it to come to me, I went after it, I pursue it with all my might, a total dedication, disciplined, can do positive attitude, with a burning desire, passion, and enthusiasm, a single minded focus, hard work, resilience, persistence, day in and day out going after what I want, until I achieved it.

My fellow readers when you decide to do this, over time, the success will be yours, much more then you ever thought or planed for. You must realize and be aware with out a purpose, and a want in life, your success and financial independence might always remain nothing but a dream, since it's very easy to get sidetracked on your life's journey. Many people do exactly that, wonder and drift through life with achieving and accomplishing very little.

By all means decide, make a choice, take action, and full responsibility. You're success, financial independence, and a better you is depending on it. Good luck.

6. All of us, at one time, or another, blame someone or something for our lack of success, be it financial, family, career, or being unhappy with life in general. Most successful people realize this and become aware of it early in life and make the necessary decisions and choices to correct it. They stop the blame game, and take full responsibility for their decisions, choices that they made and the present situation they are in right now. You can continue to blame and waste time doing it, it won't change you or your circumstances and it definitely will not put you on your road to success. To better yourself, to win, to succeed, to have the life you want, you have to acknowledge the reality, the truth, that it is you who made the decisions, you who took the actions, and made the choices that got you to your present situation, circumstances, the kind of life you are living right now.

You chose the career you are in.
You took the dead end job.
You chose not to make the change.
You didn't want to go back to school.
You chose your friends.
You listened to them.
You trusted them.
You chose to live beyond your means, and buy the things you cant afford.

You have to accept the fact that you are the one who is responsible in creating your life the way it is. Through out the book I pointed out if achieving success was easy everybody would be successful. I hope you have learned from my experiences on the long road to success and financial independence that you do run the risk of failure, being wrong, losing your hard earned money, at times feeling of being hopeless, confused, waste of time and effort. **I can tell you one thing for sure, and that is, if you don't change, take chances, or calculated risks, your life will never change for better.** It is better to try and fail then never to try.

By not trying, failure or life of mediocrity, or government dependency is inevitable. To fail it shows you have been trying, you will learn from it, and try again, and again. Failure is a stepping-stone to success, every successful person failed at one time or another at something. My hope is that you learned to accept the fact to make the right choices and take full responsibility for necessary changes, and risks you are going to take in creating the life you dreamed off, the exact life you want.

Here and now make a promise to yourself to stop blaming and complaining, but rather to get on with creating a better life, a better you. Simply forget the mistakes off the past, learn from them, and press on to the greater achievements of the future.

7. Sadly majority of us think that we could never reach the financial independence.

The good news is, that you don't have to be in that majority. I chose not to think that way, not to believe it, you read that, through out the book, and you can too.

Your choice, your decision must be absolute, with a strong belief, and self confidence that you can achieve the financial independence you seek, the point in your life that you are truly happy, satisfied, worry and debt free, with enough money and income to live the life you want, you chose, the life you desire, not them, but you. You will decide, when the time is right for you, not your boss or the government.

This is what owning a small business offers, an opportunity to achieve the financial independence to give you the freedom, a choice, to create the life you want. This is what you should have learned in reading the book, by my own experiences in owning a small business or simply just being in charge of your life, by creating the kind of life you want. You have to accept the fact that opportunities do exist to reach your financial independence and the life you want through so many channels and paths. Read the book again to see of the many jobs and businesses I have tried on my own journey to success.

Don't forget to realize and be aware of how lucky you are, and of all the advantages you have by simply being here in America. Still the land of opportunity, the land that I love, the country that millions upon millions of people all around the world hope and wish that they could be here in America.

You can copy success, from one of your relatives, friends, or your role model. Just don't give up. Remember the saying; "Winner never quits, and quitter never wins." It doesn't matter if it takes you little longer, so what if you have to work harder then ever, so what if you miss watching the super bowl, world series, or you don't go on your vacation, so what. You are focused, you are determined, you know what you want, what is important, what is a priority, you are totally clear on what matters the most to you.

You are on a mission that over time will pay off, as you reach your own financial independence along with the joyful contentment in life. I can tell you first hand from my own experience in achieving financial independence, along with a joyful contentment in life.

Financial independence has nothing to do with rich. Financial independence is the beautiful, and comforting experience of having enough. Being debt free, and having enough to live a comfortable worry free life, and to live it the way you want. Reaching a point of having enough is happy, comfortable, fearless, worry free, a trusting, honest, proud, relaxed, flexible, free, joyful and content place to be.

HE WHO KNOWS HE HAS ENOUGH IS TRULY RICH.[5]

I wish, you reach your point of having enough, to be able to enjoy it with your loved ones as I have.

---

5 'Your Money or Your Life' by Vicki Robin and Joe Dominguez

8. You have learned from reading the book that you definitely do not need a college degree to own a business or to be successful. Don't get me wrong; in no way, shape, or form am I trying to knock a college education. All I am saying is that you don't need it, to own a business, be self-employed, and be successful in life. People who are smart, informative, and have many different experiences do have a great advantage over people who don't. To acquire the knowledge you need, to become successful, is to copy successful people. Find a role model, attend special classes, training programs, seminars, and read the books such as this one. The books on self-improvement, motivational books, books on lives of great people, and books on starting a small business.

When was the last time you went to the library?

It's your tax dollars that build and keep the libraries open, so use them. I know we have the internet and other modern technologies to get the information you want, but for me and millions of others a trip to a library is always fun, a little adventure, a new discovery, a joy of finding a special book, and the anticipation of going home and reading it.

Buy a business were the individual seller or the company will provide all the training you need to succeed. Similar to what I have explained in the book regarding the Route Business. While you read the book, you should have realized, and be aware, that your success depends more on you, then the knowledge you have about the business. What I mean, by you, is the way you think, your work habit, your attitude, discipline, confidence, persistence, reliability, direction, your personal responsibility, and so on. All of these have to work together in line towards your plans, your goals, your wants, and the life you want to have. These are building blocks, a foundation, and stepping-stones, for any success you wish to achieve. When you acquire them, when you are in total disciplined control of them, and use them every day, then you can easily learn any specialized skills and the knowledge, you know that you will need, to make your plans, goals, and the life you want to become a reality.

9. After reading the book, I hope you have decided that you no longer have to live from paycheck to paycheck. Yes you can develop the discipline, and plan on how to save money.

I shoved and proved it to you, through out the book, especially in the chapter on; Ways to save money for a purchase of small business. If there is a will there is a way to solve most if not all of your; problems, situations, circumstances, that are preventing and holding you back in creating the life you want for yourself, and your family. Your will, desire, discipline, attitude, confidence and the actions you take have to work together day in and day out, towards your plans, goals, and wants you have decided on. You have to take charge and accept the full responsibility for your present circumstances, with a deep desire to make the necessary changes in you behavior, habits, and actions, to be able to reach positive results and the outcome you desire and want.

Example; you may want to save three hundred dollars a week?

At the end of the year you would have saved 15600.00 dollars. In three years you may have enough for a down payment on a small Route Business.
How are you going to save the three hundred dollars a week?

1. Work longer hours, or get a part time job?
2. Cut back on your spending the money?
3. Why not try to use both options, to work for you and your plans and dreams.

There just might be a way for you to buy that small business much sooner rather the later.

Write all of your options down, and pick the one's that can best work for you, to be able to reach the results and the outcomes that you want and you decided on. After you have done this, you may discover, that it may be possible for you to save much more money every week, even double that amount of three hundred dollars a week. When you make the tough decisions, you have to follow up with disciplined actions to make it work for you.

You automatically empower yourself and boost your confidence level along with an attitude that develops, and becomes a positive can-do attitude. This will open up a new world to you, with new possibilities, more opportunities, more and better choices, all because, you chose to make the tough decisions, accept to make the necessary sacrifices, with a lot of hard work for a better tomorrow, for a better future, for a better you. You have proved to yourself that you are indeed ready, willing, and able to do what ever is necessary, what ever it takes to be in charge of your life. This is the only way that you can start creating and working towards the life you desire, things you want to accomplish, and things you want to have, when you are in charge, and take full responsibility.

10. My fellow readers majority of the successful people that I know don't waste their time reading, listening, or watching the big negative media that's all around us, with a tremendous impact and influence on how people think and behave. They all try to entertain, and sell us stuff, with out any regard, for it's truthfulness and is it really good for us or not. They push, and constantly bombard us with promises of instant riches by gambling, in casinos, or buying lottery tickets. Get rich quick, seminars, workshops, with Hollywood looking, fast talkers, trying to separate you from your hard earned money. By selling you unrealistic, unreachable dreams, with empty promises and blatant lies, all while trying to protect themselves with the very complex, and difficult to understand, and see, fine print. Get rich quick programs, and seminars such as; day trading stocks, buying properties with little or no money down, or to get rich of properties in foreclosure, and many others.

Mostly, irresponsible, negative media, and the pharmaceutical industry, promises us, instant cure, for just about anything that ails us. Just ask your doctor about this medicine. Take the medicine, making sure you finish it completely and all what ails you, is gone. Never mind of so many side affects, that in too many cases will get you sick, that you need different kind of medicine to treat the side affects.

How about every day of negative reporting like; the economy is bad, unemployment is high, crime is out of control, there is no good jobs, forget about starting your own business now, blame everyone and everything for lack of success and quality of life.

There is very little positive news told or written about. Period. The positive news, that you can actually use in every day living, to make the positive decisions and choices to be a better, and more successful you. Instead, if you keep listening, watching, and reading, the every day negative, all about profit driven media, its news and stories that they tell us, advertise, and constantly slam us with it, you get to believe it.

My friends, if majority of us didn't accept it, bought into their negative stories, messages, and lies they would not continue to keep pushing it and selling it every day, with more aggressiveness, more blatant lies, empty promises, in their agenda, to enrich themselves and take advantage of our many weaknesses, as they are master exploiters, and unfortunately most of us continue to listen, to believe them, and buy what ever they push on us, which puts further strains on our finances and our lives.

THE MESSAGE OF MY BOOK IS TO EDUCATE YOU, IN THINKING, AND BEING AWARE AT ALL TIMES, WHAT IS IN YOUR BEST INTEREST, TO EMPOWER YOUR, TO HELP YOU, HELP YOURSELF, TO MAKE THE NECESSARY POSITIVE CHANGES, TO BE A LEADER, NOT A FOLLOWER, TO THINK FOR YOURSELF, TO BE BOLD, AND GO AFTER YOUR DREAMS, AND ASPIRATIONS.

I know you can succeed, that you can, own a small business; there is always opportunities out there for people who keep looking, and never quit searching, striving, training to be better.

Small business man, entrepreneur's, go-getters, innovators, investors, with their own hard work, and many sacrifices build this great country of ours. To keep America strong, and the kind of country, that smaller countries, (The Emerging Democracies) around the Globe can look up to, for our know-how and leadership.

We all have to make a concentrated effort, a real positive difference, in reversing the trend of far too many of our fellow citizens every day, more and more tend to rely on many of our subsidized programs. So many programs, that I care not to write about, since it's mostly negative, and downright un- American.

What ever happened to personal responsibility, self-reliance, pulling your own weight, personal pride, in your work, and your accomplishments?

Your Thinking And Beliefs After Reading This Book?

You now have, a genuine opportunity, to join in, keeping America the greatest country in the world, by becoming a business owner, entrepreneur, innovator, investor, mentor, hard worker, independent, self reliant and proud of all your efforts and successes.

Not only will you improve your own life and your family's life, but you will also help our country, and our way of life.

Winners are people like you. They make the world a better place to be. May God bless you, and the U.S.A.

What we think or what we know or what we believe is, in the end, of little consequence. The only consequence is what we do.

John Ruskin - English Author

Chapter 30
CONCLUDING THOUGHTS.

Through out the book I tried my best to introduce you to the Route Business, and to make a positive difference in your life. I strongly believe in telling it like it is, and that being successful and working for yourself is not easy. There is no perfect job or a perfect business. In explaining and teaching you about the route business, I believe I did not painted a rosy picture, or sugar coat anything, just simply gave my best effort to tell you like it is, nothing more and nothing less.

For thousands and thousands of hard working route business owners across this great country of ours, it's simply a great business to be in, especially last several years and continuing, with an issue of job security and fair wages in a tough economy.

Now, it's all up to you.

The ball is in your corner.

THE GOOD NEWS IS, THAT YOU HAVE A COMPLETE CONTROL OF YOUR THOUGHTS, HABITS, DECISIONS, ACTIONS AND INACTIONS YOU TAKE. WE HAVE THIS GREAT POWER, WHICH WE TAKE FOR GRANTED, AND RARELY STOP AND THINK ABOUT.

Reflection of our lives depends on the choices we make.

To have a better life, simply make better choices.

Concluding Thoughts.

Working for someone else is like going to the gym five times a week, but your boss gains all the muscle.

In any business, it's all about the time period, and the effort you put in. It's when you're not trying to get rich quick that you get rich slowly.

I thank you for your interest,
and wish you best of luck.

May God bless you in all your endeavors?
Sincerely

If you have any questions or comments, email routetosuccess1@gmail.com

Chapter 31
LIST OF MAJOR COMPANIES THAT SELL ROUTES/DISTRIBUTORSHIPS

Some companies may not be selling their products nationally but only regionally. This is the reason that I wrote that when you are ready to start looking to purchase a route business to contact companies directly, but also contact local route brokers. They generally have many years of experience, and knowledge of the local market. They know about the sales in the area and the prices for certain route businesses. Price for the same name brand route does vary substantially from region to region and at times from different areas that are not to far from each other. You can't forget the supply and demand issue.

Route Brokers in many instances have listings of smaller local companies as well as companies starting out with route business program and the nationally famous brand name routes such as these;

Pepperidge Farm
Snapple
Boars Head
Fed Ex
Tropicana
Mistic Beverages
Vitamin Water

Dannon Yogurt
Snyders Pretzels
Thumans
Tasty cake
Martins Potato Rolls
Diets&Watson
Herr's Snacks

List of Major Companies that sell routes/distributorships

Arnold Bread	Bellacicco Bread
Stella Doro Cookies	Kettle Brand
Archway Cookies	UTZ Snacks
Keebler Cookies	Bachman Snacks
Wise Snacks	Pechters Bread
Mission Foods	Mr. Softee
Edy's Ice Cream	Nantucket Nectars

I wish you best of luck on you journey to independence, job security, flexible schedule, and a lot of hard work with financial security as your reward, and so much more.

Keep the book handy and read it over and over to fully understand it's message and at the same time you will realize that it can save and help you make more money then you ever thought in this great business for owner/operator.

ABOUT AUTHOR

Bozidar Barry Strk is a route business expert as well as a small rental property owner/manager. He is a realist, with a common sense approach in starting your own business, without the empty promises of quick and easy riches that anybody can achieve. His mission, his purpose, and the goal is; to help, guide, teach, motivate, inspire, and set a positive example through his experience, to all the individuals with a can-do attitude, discipline, and personal responsibility, to work, create, and build a better tomorrow for themselves and their family.

These are the individuals who make a world a better place to be for you and for me.

You are invited to join them.

It's never too late to start, these are

the individuals who want

and dare to take charge of their future, be in charge of their life, and create the kind of life that they want, hope, dream, and wish for.

As far back as I can remember, I always loved to work, build, create, and be active. Route Business and my part time small rental property business provided me with this opportunity. Not only to the things that I loved, but at the same time earn a good income and more importantly build equity, build wealth, slowly and securely over time.

My fellow readers we know that most jobs don't provide us with such an opportunity for you and your family. Since both businesses were good to me, and my family, I said to myself; "Why not help other individuals learn about these small business opportunities."

(Book on my experience in owning and managing small rental properties will be coming in the near future.)

It's an opportunity to take control of your own job and income security, which in turn lets you control your own future.

Please, just imagine for a moment that for next ten, twenty years or more you don't have to be concerned about job and income security for you and your family. Having that peace of mind is priceless, for most of us, especially in today's job market. How about the freedom, and independence in deciding how many days and hours you want to work, and the kind of life you wish to build, for you and your family.

The purpose of the book is not only to introduce you to the Route Business, but to empower, motivate, inspire, and show you, that yes you can own, and succeed in small business of your own. The right small business ownership can transform your life for better. Owning a Route Business you are in the business for yourself, but not by yourself. You will have the power of a billion dollars brand name corporation behind you, every step of the way. You are part of the team. Your success is also their success.

I hope that you enjoyed the book and read it over often to stay positive and motivated on your route to success.

Success in life is when people benefit from your actions.

My wish is that a great number of people really do benefit from the book, and that they learn to make better choices in life, as well as necessary changes to live a better, more successful, more meaningful life, that they can in turn inspire others as millions of people are searching for good advice on how to live a better life, find a better job or run a better business.

My sincere best wishes for your journey on "Your Route To Success".

www.ingramcontent.com/pod-product-compliance
Lightning Source LLC
Chambersburg PA
CBHW051704170526
45167CB00002B/534